Praise for *The Churning, Inner Leadership*

"Brilliant... Fundamental... Entertaining... The inspiring manual to improve our ability to cope and thrive in post-normal VUCA times. Extremely wise... Desperately needed... Highly recommended... Helps to turn this seemingly scary-looking future to become an adventure full of possibilities."

    – Ilkka Kakko, serial entrepreneur, Finland

"An essential shift in thinking; an ethical framework for business decision makers based on emotional maturity."

    – Joshua Englander, Business Director, MRM McCann, Germany

"Essential reading for any leader who wants to thrive in times of change... An easy read... with the potential for real personal change in developing authentic leadership."

    – Kate Cooper, Head of Research, Policy & Standards, Institute of Leadership and Management, London

"An outstanding book. Inspirational and uplifting. A beacon of light."

    – Giovanni Facchinetti, Managing Director, B4B, Switzerland

"My favourite book to turn to when I have a leadership dilemma."

    – Emma Richardson, Director of HR Consultancy Services, Lewis Silkin, London

"Should be on every change-maker's bookshelf. A rich compendium of extremely practical exercises and guidance... Easy to read... Detailed and clearly explained... 21st century leadership... Invaluable."

    – Simon Robinson, co-founder Holonomics Education, Brazil

"It's brilliant! I keep dipping into it and finding little pearls of wisdom. The toolbox for taking control [and] leading the life you want."

— Sally Birch, writer and artist, England

"Refreshing and necessary. A personal development journey recommended for anyone aspiring to refocus their energies in today's highly unpredictable world."

— Eric Lynn, organisation development consultant, Germany

"An excellent guide to riding the waves of change and being stronger when faced with adversity. A practical guide to coping with uncertainty and change."

— Peter Cook, leadership and innovation consultant, England

"An outstanding book… very much enjoying reading it… A very useful map to navigate the VUCA world we are living in. In these difficult times, we need to find an internal compass, represented by our values, our purpose, and what resonates deep inside of us. [This] book is a very valuable companion for those who follow their inspiration and dare to venture out of the beaten path in search of meaning."

— Reader on Amazon.com

"Excellent: tools for building leadership in times of change. It's clear, pragmatic, practical, radical."

— Reader on Twitter

THE CHURNING

Volume 1:

INNER LEADERSHIP

Tools for Building Inspiration in Times of Change

Also by Finn Jackson

The Escher Cycle: Creating Self-Reinforcing Business Advantage

THE CHURNING

Volume 1:
INNER LEADERSHIP

Tools for Building Inspiration
In Times of Change

Finn Jackson

Hertford Street Press

For my children
and your children
and for our children's children

With grateful thanks for their encouragement and support to:

Andrew Montgomery, Barley Jackson, Betty Lim, Carin Jackson,
Caspar Henderson, Chris Dalton, Christian Wolf, Daniel Doherty,
Ed Dowding, Ellen Stegers, Emma Richardson,
Gary Waterworth-Owen, George Simpson, Giovanni Facchinetti,
Ilkka Kakko, Jenny Andersson, John Kellden, Julia Lockwood,
Karen Arthur, Kate Colquhoun, Kenneth Enright, Lauren Roman,
Lise Bulloch, Mark Pritchard, Mitzi Blennerhassett, Neil Burston, Nicci
Shepherd, Patrick Andrews, Paula Burgess, Peter Furtado, Pete Coates,
Ramkumar Nagabushanam, Rob Barnard-Weston, Sally Birch, Scooter,
Sharon Ede, Sheila Harrison, and Suzanne Enright.

CONTENTS

PREFACE TO THE SECOND EDITION

In the 15 months since this book was published the need for it has grown. Last year saw not just one but two leading G7 countries shift from stability to increased volatility under the isolationist policies of Donald Trump and Brexit. North Korea emerged unexpectedly as a long range nuclear power, and the leaderships of Saudi Arabia, Zimbabwe, and Burma/Myanmar all took unexpected paths.

At the same time, the global economy returned to significant growth for the first time since 2008. Cryptocurrencies such as Bitcoin emerged as new sources of value (but not stability), inequality grew, and extreme weather in the form of hurricanes, floods, and forest fires caused damage running into hundreds of billions of dollars.

Technology continued to disrupt our lives. The political impacts of fake news delivered via social media became clearer and the move towards driverless vehicles accelerated. At the end of the year, #metoo and Australian flu both swept the world unexpectedly. And then, in early 2018, small swarms of drones attacked Russian forces in Syria.

It is becoming harder than ever to predict what tomorrow will bring. This second edition contains colour diagrams, some edits for clarity, and an expanded description of the implications of *Inner Leadership* (personal joy, organisational advantage, and a more stable world). So whether you want to make clearer sense of the world, build your emotional intelligence, find more options for moving forward, inspire yourself and others to do what needs to be done, find your life purpose, develop twenty-first century leadership, or simply learn how to stay calm in a crisis, this book has the tools and techniques for you.

Finn Jackson
Oxford, January 2018

FOREWORD

I met Finn Jackson the spring of 1999 when he arrived in my office in Telford, England. I liked him the minute we met. Some people are like that: you know at the time you meet them they will be there for the duration of your life. Meeting Finn was like that for me.

At the time, we both worked for Electronic Data Systems (EDS). Finn was a strategist working on pan-European accounts. I was a Human Resources executive managing the transition of 2,000 British civil servants into EDS, as part of a ten-year, $10bn contract. Four years into the transition, our culture change program had been highly successful. We had significantly reduced staff turnover, increased customer satisfaction, and signed millions in additional business. Finn had come to learn what had made the transition so successful.

In our meeting we talked about what makes significant culture change work: what motivates people to change, why leaders change, as well as why they won't, and how to create sustainable organizational change. Those late 1990s were the beginning of the dot-com era, so what we also talked about was how startups like Amazon could create a vision that would get people to leap out of bed excited to go to work. That conversation and the many others Finn and I have had since were about how to create inspiring leadership in times of constant and accelerated change, or what Finn calls 'the churning'. And that is what this book is about.

What happened next for me also turned out to be a great time of churning. I wish I had had the tools in this book to help me through the transition I went through in the three years after I met Finn. EDS hired a new CEO whose focus was not on creating vision and culture change but on cutting costs. I returned to the US and to Silicon Valley, where I started a leadership coaching and consulting company, and spent the next 15 years working in Asia, helping multinational clients develop their leaders.

In 2000 Finn became a client of mine. Soon after he left EDS to write his first book and start his own consultancy. But as Finn would be the first to tell you, life doesn't always go as planned. He faced his own transition as he stepped back from the corporate world, left a long marriage, lost a parent, and faced a life-threatening illness. I'll leave it to Finn to tell the details of his story. What's important for you is the result, this book.

There are other books that contain elements of what is in this one. But what makes this book unique, and why I am honored to be writing this foreword, is the clarity and ease with which Finn weaves and synthesizes the different elements together into an integrated process. The tools he describes will help you make sense of the changes around you, find the best way forward for you, and stay centered and grounded even when the frequency and velocity of the changes around you may seem overwhelming.

The result is a way to find your purpose and values, then put them into practice. It shows how to articulate your vision in a way that inspires others to want to go along with you. And, in the end, *Inner Leadership* is also about how to combine culture change with strategy to create a new kind of enterprise, designed to succeed in a churning world.

At its core, this book is about what to do when things around you seem to be moving too quickly or falling apart. Finn might not describe it that way, but fundamentally that is what it's about: how to develop the ability not only to survive but to thrive in times of ubiquitous change, and how to teach the people you lead to do the same, as together you create the organizations we will all want to be part of in the future.

Suzanne Enright
President
Kensu Leadership Group, Inc.

INTRODUCTION

We are living through a time of unprecedented global change, a time I call 'The Churning'.

You probably already know what I am talking about, but for clarity here are just some of the specific issues, trends, and drivers that are already impacting our organisations and us, both as public leaders and as private individuals:

The banking crisis, the Euro crisis, Grexit, Brexit, austerity, taxation; social unrest, the rise of the political right and left, armed conflict, terrorism, war, mass migration, immigration; the price and availability of basic resources (think oil, steel, water, food); new technologies (think smartphones, drones, artificial intelligence, Internet of things, GMOs, biomimicry, driverless vehicles, solar power) and disruptive innovation (Uber, Airbnb, Tesla); high competition, low economic growth, stock market volatility; mass shootings, gang rapes, storms, floods, droughts, earthquakes, capsizing ferries, missing planes, new diseases (of plants, animals, and humans), climate change, and the ongoing degradation of the planetary life support system we call "the environment."

Just ten years ago most of these items were barely on our radar. Now they are the new normal. And although there may be some items on this list you have not heard of, and others you do not care about, there is probably at least one item here that is already affecting you significantly. The issues are wide-ranging but connected, and we all have our own specific take on what The Churning means to us.

As well as the direct impacts on us and our organisations, there are also the indirect impacts we experience via customers, suppliers, and employees. In 2011, for example, severe floods hit electronics suppliers in Thailand. The resulting local disruption was a major factor in Japan's Sony Corporation quickly reversing its global profit forecast of $0.8bn, made just weeks before, into a predicted loss of $1.2bn. Less dramatically, the price of food might seem irrelevant to your business, but food prices affect the remaining disposable income for all other consumer goods, which affects profits in consumer industries, which then affects priorities and spend in B2B. And an employee who is worrying about making ends meet is a less productive employee.

We have created a more interdependent and connected world, and as globalisation progresses so the proverbial butterfly's wing on one side of the planet really can cause a storm on the other. We cannot predict precisely what will happen when, but our qualitative daily experience tells us that the world is becoming more complex and unpredictable, rather than more stable.

This combined uncertainty and lack of control affects us all emotionally, especially those of us who, as leaders, are held responsible and accountable for delivering results in a churning world. So, as well as the outer turmoil of the physical world, we can also experience an inner turmoil in our emotional world.

As private individuals we now have direct access to the most extreme stories from anywhere in the world, 24 hours a day. At best this can become a background 'drip, drip, drip' that unconsciously heightens or numbs our emotional state. At worst, depending on the extent to which we or someone close to us has been affected directly, it can impact our ability to contribute to our team and to get the job done.

The people we work with – customers, suppliers, colleagues, and employees – all have their pressures too. And when two pressured people meet it is no surprise if stressed communications lead to poor decisions, making a bad situation worse. In this way the churning feeds on itself and grows.

This time I call the churning is a time of volatility, uncertainty, complexity, and ambiguity that exists both in the outer world of physical events and the inner world of our imagination and emotions.

It won't last forever. It is a transitional phase to something better, as you will understand by the time you finish this book. But to reach that point we need new thinking, new frameworks, and new tools for leading both ourselves and others.

What Is Leadership?

If we are looking for a new kind of leadership, one that enables us to take effective action in a world we can't predict or control, then we have to start by asking ourselves, "What do we mean by 'leadership'?"

The dictionary defines leadership as "the action of leading a group of people or an organisation, or the ability to do this." At the simplest level, this has to start from leading an organisation of just one person: ourselves.

In this book, leadership is not about whether you have a formal position in an organisation or how many people report to you. Leadership here is about an attitude of mind: the decision to make sense of your world and then shape it to achieve whatever matters most to you. You are the leader of yourself. And if you want to thrive in this new time of churning it is essential that you learn new skills for achieving that better, and then expand from there.

In which case, what does it take to lead well in a time of change?

The essence of great leadership, I believe, is about delivering two things: inspiration and results. The greatest leaders are the ones who inspire us the most. The greatest leaders are also the ones who deliver the best results. The truly great leaders are the ones who somehow manage to deliver both inspiration and results.

To reflect this *The Churning* has been divided into two volumes.

One volume focuses on execution and results, or what I call 'outer leadership'. This is about finding new ways to understand the business context, identify risks, opportunities, and key success factors, then chart the critical path forward. It's about building and managing the business not as a machine but as a living organism that adapts and evolves in a time of change. That volume is currently under development.

The other volume, which you are reading now, is about creating inspiration. This is 'inner leadership' and it involves strengthening our abilities in a range of skills, from keeping calm in a crisis to finding more opportunities in any situation, to converting the best of them into a vision that inspires us and others to move forward and do what needs to be done. It is about understanding, managing, and generating the emotional responses we want, in ourselves and other people.

Both halves of leadership are important so where do we begin?

At first glance it might seem to make sense to start with outer leadership. After all, we urgently need to address the crises we face, and only after we have done so will we really have time for all this 'emotion' and 'inspiration' stuff.

But there will always be another crisis. And crisis creates stress, which means that people don't see the situation clearly, stress each other out even more, and take poor decisions, which they then implement badly. The crisis doesn't get resolved, and the churning deepens, or at best gets "kicked down the road" for a while.

If we start instead with inner leadership we will be able to see our current situations more clearly and more calmly. We will be more certain about what we want to create instead, and more able to articulate that as an inspiring vision. Then when we come to outer leadership, our implementation will be more focused, more enthusiastic: more efficient, effective, and adaptable to changing circumstances. And that will create results that last.

Whether we want to change the state the world is in, or simply lead ourselves and our organisations through that world more successfully, we have to start with inner leadership. After all, how can we expect to lead others if we can't first lead ourselves?

Or, think about it this way: when you're on a plane and the oxygen masks drop down, every single pre-flight safety check tells you exactly the same thing, "Put on your own oxygen mask first, secure it, and breathe normally before helping others with theirs."

This book will give you the tools to 'put your own oxygen mask in place' by finding a vision that inspires you. You will then be ready to help others with theirs and move forward together to create whatever results you want: inspired by your vision and secure in the knowledge that you will be able to face any challenge that arises.

This is *Inner Leadership*.

Seven Steps to Inner Leadership

Inner leadership involves a range of skills that are applicable under different circumstances. Different readers will come to this book with some skills already in place, and with strengths and weaknesses in different areas. In writing this book I want to provide two things.

First, I want to provide a set of practical tools that enable anyone to improve their levels of performance and confidence in each area. So, where you are already strong, I want to provide world-class tools that enable you to improve further. And where you are weak, I want to provide tools that are clear and straightforward enough for anyone to use.

Second, I want to provide a structure that arranges the skills in order. There is no point trying to run before you can walk, and there is no point trying to climb the fifth step on a staircase before you have reached the fourth. By showing all the steps in order I want to provide a structure and a context for inner leadership that reveals the entire process, enables you to identify any current weaknesses and missing links, and empowers you to climb the whole staircase more quickly, even if starting from the beginning.

Altogether there are seven areas of skill, competence, and ability that combine to form the capabilities of inner leadership.

The first is to build a strong foundation. This enables you to remain calm during times of crisis, and when times are stable to extend and expand your leadership influence and reach.

The second is to make clear sense of your situation. When the world no longer works the way it used to it can be easy to misinterpret events. This second area of competence is about identifying the mistaken assumptions we can easily make in a time of change, and about developing new ways of recognising what is really going on.

The third important capability is to be able to identify the full range of opportunities in any situation. Not only does this expand your options for moving forward, but it also brings you a greater feeling of control and a more positive attitude.

The fourth skill lies in choosing which of the available opportunities to pursue. In a time of churning, it might seem best to move forward in whichever direction is easiest, but this can lead you down blind alleys. It also denies your ability to shape the world. Knowing where you want to get to in the long run enables you to choose the short-term opportunities that will take you in that direction. It also gives you the stability, confidence, and inspiration to pivot and tack from time to time (if you need to), knowing that your overall destination remains unchanged.

The fifth competency comes from defining two key yardsticks: your purpose and your values. Tactically, these tell you which issues matter to you, which to ignore, and how to respond. (This increases your adaptability and agility in a changing world.) Strategically, your purpose and values provide a litmus test for deciding the attractiveness of new opportunities. (This brings consistency and direction.) And as with the previous skills, this competency also strengthens your foundation and builds towards greater inspiration.

The sixth competency lies at the heart of inner leadership. It is the ability to describe the opportunity or direction you have chosen in a way that inspires you and other people to want to make it happen. When everything is changing, people can often feel uncertain and afraid. Inspiration gives us the courage to shift into action and the energy and enthusiasm to sustain that action over time.

Finally, the seventh key skill is the ability to address the inner leadership challenges that will inevitably arise as you work to make your vision a reality – and to do so in a way that turns those challenges to your advantage, maintaining and growing the levels of inspiration you have created.

Seven Capabilities of Inner Leadership

1. Build Strong Foundation

2. Make Sense of Situation

3. Find More Opportunities

4. Choose Best Way Forward

5. Know Your Purpose & Values

6. Create Inspiring Vision

7. Prepare for Implement- ation

These seven skills or capabilities are laid out in seven chapters. Each builds on what has come before and adds depth to what comes after. So, although it is possible to jump ahead to start in any chapter, you will find that you develop deeper and longer-lasting responses to each step if you take the chapters in order.

Once you have completed all seven chapters you will also find that the work of Chapters 1 and 2 becomes easier. Completing and repeating this cycle of inner leadership is how you teach yourself more about who you are, what matters most to you, and how to achieve that with least effort.

Measurement

Measurement is an important part of every leader's life, both for defining the objectives you are working towards and for calculating progress towards them.

The outcomes of inner leadership are more difficult to measure than many others but I don't see why they should be any different. You need to know whether reading and applying this book is making a difference for you and I want to ensure that it does. So I have defined a measurement system that you can use to track the impact that the book is having.

You can apply that using your own notebook. Alternatively, you can purchase the *Inner Leadership Workbook*: a large format paperback containing tables for recording your answers to all the tools and exercises. Finally, the workbook can also be downloaded as a free e-book from www.thechurning.net/p4913/.

Of course, as any parent with young children being tested in school knows, metrics are never an end in themselves: they are only an approximation, an indicator or a proxy for something more important. In the same way, good leadership is fundamentally unmeasurable, and yet we all know it when we see it.

Remember this as you apply the measurement system. It is just an indicator of something more important, not an end in itself.

This book defines seven skills or competencies of inner leadership. Carried out in the right order, they combine to form a ladder or a staircase that enables us to climb from wherever we are now to create an inspiring vision of what we want instead and prepare to implement that vision.

At the lowest level, if some disaster has just happened, we might be experiencing extreme inner turmoil or 'Churning'.

We can use the tools of Chapter 1 to move our inner state to become 'Centred' and then 'Grounded'.

Chapter 2 helps us to make sense of the situation. It gives us greater confidence about what is happening. We can call the inner emotional state we experience here 'Sure'.

Chapter 3 enables us to realise that every challenge is an opportunity. Identifying these opportunities makes us feel 'Optimistic' about moving forward. Then in Chapter 4 we choose the direction of the opportunity that suits us best: we become 'Directed'.

In Chapters 5 and 6 we identify our priorities and create an inspiring vision. Our emotional states here become 'Determined' and then 'Inspired'.

Chapter 7 brings us the competencies that make us 'Ready' to move forward into action and outer leadership.

All this is illustrated in the following diagram.

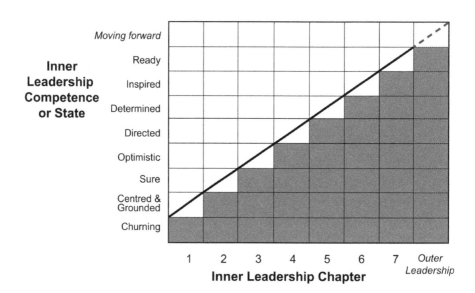

Measuring Inner Leadership

In this way the skills of inner leadership enable us to raise our inner emotional states from Churning to Centred, Grounded, Sure, Optimistic, Directed, Determined, Inspired, and then Ready to move to action. Once we can do this for ourselves then we can do it for other people.

This book is a set of tools for understanding, managing, and generating the emotional states we want, in ourselves and others.

For each step we can rate our ability on a scale of 0 to 10. We will do this at the beginning and end of each chapter.

Review this now. Do you see any of the stages as being particular strengths or weaknesses for you? Are you equally strong throughout? Do you have weaknesses in one area that prevent you from fully *cycling through* the process of inner leadership, holding back your learning and improvement over time? In which chapters do you expect to gain the most and least benefit? Where do you most want to improve? Where will you begin? Record your answers in your workbook.

As you work through this book you can expect that different chapters will bring you different levels of challenge and benefit. You can also expect to increase your performance at every stage.

Each step on its own has been designed to be small, simple, and straightforwardly easy. Combined in the order presented here, they become a transformational spiral staircase that anyone can climb.

Reading Alone Is Not Enough

Please don't read this book. Or rather, please don't *only* read it. You also need to do the work.

Reading *Inner Leadership* will bring you benefits, it is true, but you do not learn to swim by reading a book about swimming.

Inner Leadership has been designed to be a very practical approach. It is a 'what' and a 'why' book and also very much a 'how to' book. It contains a series of specially-chosen tools and exercises, arranged in a developmental order that builds step by step.

To get the full value you need to find *your* answers to these questions. You need to apply the tools to uncover *your* insights into *your* specific situation. That might take time, so the paperback and electronic workbooks have been provided to make it easier for you to record and track your progress. You can also use your own notebook.

Go at your own speed. A chapter per month might well be appropriate to bed in and establish some of the tools and techniques.

Do this, and by the end of the process you will have gained new skills and insights that improve the way you lead yourself and others during times of change. You will have found your solutions to the issues you face and created a clear roadmap to guide you through this time of churning.

Remember that different tools will be useful for different people at different times. So as you work your way through the book, expect to find some tools more useful than others. Remember that each step builds towards what comes later, so do try out all the tools at least once, especially on your first pass. And remember also that inner leadership is a repeating, circular process of continuous improvement across all seven competencies, so tools that seem less useful today may well become more useful tomorrow, either for you or for someone else you know. It will be better if you have learned and practiced them before you need them urgently.

A visitor to New York once asked, "How do you get to Carnegie Hall?" The answer, of course, is "Practice, practice, practice."

The tools and techniques in this book will enable you to identify and then lead yourself to *your equivalent* of Carnegie Hall. But only if you *practice* them.

Five Levels of Benefit

By developing these seven sets of inner leadership competencies we can expect to see benefits on five levels.

First, if we apply just one or two sets of tools we will solve the immediate problems we face in this time of churning. We'll remain calm in a wider range of circumstances, find more alternative ways forward, express our objectives in more inspiring ways, and so on.

Second, if we apply all the tools in order then we will become more inspirational leaders of ourselves and other people. Applied in order, the tools provide a seven-step framework for responding to any situation that arises:

1. Steady yourself and connect deeply with who you are and what matters most to you
2. Make clear sense of the situation
3. Find the opportunities
4. Choose the opportunity that is best for you
5. Check it against your purpose and values
6. Describe your chosen way forward as an inspiring vision
7. Prepare for implementation

As we repeat this process we become better at it. We become more sure of our direction, more practiced and more confident in our ability to move there under any circumstances. We become able to choose our response to any situation. We become what Nassim Nicholas Taleb calls 'antifragile'.

Things (and people) that break when placed under stress, we call fragile. Things and people that survive under stress we call resilient, strong, or robust. And things and people that actually become stronger when placed under stress, Taleb calls antifragile.

This antifragility has two parts. First it is about being able to choose how we respond to a situation. (This is inner leadership.) Second it is about being able to put that response into practice in a changing world. (This is outer leadership.)

Once we develop these capabilities in ourselves as leaders, then we can apply them to direct the resources of our organisations. Then those organisations, too, can become antifragile. And an organisation that "becomes stronger when placed under stress" has competitive advantage. It becomes truly 'sustainable'.

This is the third level of benefit we can expect to see from inner leadership: the creation of more competitive, antifragile, truly sustainable leaders and organisations. People and firms with new energy, built around a strong set of purpose, values, attitudes, and behaviours, that not only cope with the stresses of this time of churning but actively use them to clarify what is important to them and improve their ability to achieve that.

By the end of this book you will have learned the inner leadership skills needed to make that happen for you, and seen how to combine them with outer leadership to become antifragile.

This leaves the fourth and fifth levels of benefits.

Einstein told us that we cannot expect to solve a problem with the same level of thinking that created it. To a degree, many of the problems we face in the world today are the direct result of our previous models of leadership. If, in the past, we'd had a different understanding of what it means to be a leader then we would have taken different decisions and we would not now be facing some of the problems that we are.

In this sense, this time of churning is really a signal to us that there is something missing in the way we currently think about what it means to be a leader. The problems we face are symptoms of our own thinking, showing us where we have opportunities to improve.

As we learn the tools and techniques needed to become better leaders in the face of these problems, so we can expect the problems themselves to begin to resolve. Instead of volatility and uncertainty, our new approach to leadership will generate a world of dynamic stability.

This is the fourth level of benefit.

The fifth level, finally, is joy. This is something we don't often talk about in business, but perhaps we should. Because your joy shows you where your purpose and values lie, and when you are working on something in line with your purpose and values you feel joy.

Purpose and values, as we shall see, are the key essential links to achieving the antifragility and radical competitive advantage we just talked about. They are also part of what we desire most as human beings: if your work is aligned with your purpose and values, in pursuit of a vision that inspires you, as part of an organisation that enables you to achieve more than you could on your own, what more is there?

The resulting joy we feel is the fifth level of benefit you can expect to achieve from applying the tools in this book.

To summarise, at one level the challenges we face today are a problem to be solved. But at another level they are also an opportunity to develop new skills and abilities and a new kind of leadership.

By applying the tools laid out in this book we can expect to become more competitive, more inspiring, and more able to choose our responses under any circumstances. We become antifragile, truly sustainable. And as more leaders and organisations acquire these skills, we can expect the symptoms of the churning itself to fade away.

Ultimately, the tools in this book provide a way for all of us to become more connected with who we are, clearer about what we care about most, and more able to achieve our purpose and joy.

Let's begin.

Inner Leadership Overview

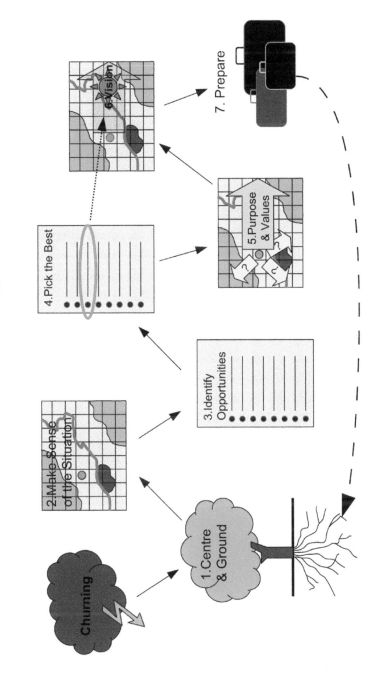

1. Centre, Ground, and Deepen

You might feel you want to jump straight in, to find your purpose and values or uncover an exciting new way forward. But the first step of inner leadership is less dramatic than that. It is at once both deceptively simple and incredibly important. It is the ability in any situation to bring ourselves back to a state of calm inner balance, then focus and connect strongly with who we are and what is most important to us. This lays the foundation for everything else that follows.

Like the roots of a tree, our ability to centre and ground is what keeps us upright when storms are raging and nourished during a drought. And when times are calm it determines how far we are able to spread the branches of our leadership out into larger challenges and roles. For this reason, it is worth spending the time to build our foundation deep and wide. This is the only chapter that recommends a daily practice for continual improvement.

The chapter has three sections.

The first describes techniques that we can use to remove or release any inner churning we might be experiencing. This gets us centred.

The second shows us how to reconnect with who we are and what matters most to us. This gets us grounded.

The third section describes how to deepen that grounded state, increasing our self-awareness and self-knowledge. This not only keeps us more centred in a wider range of circumstances, but also shows us the directions in which it will be most valuable and rewarding for us to expand our leadership influence.

Together, these three steps form the foundation on which the rest of your inner leadership will be built. Time spent on the tools in this chapter will be repaid many times over when you come to do the work of the later chapters. And the work of those chapters will reinforce and expand the foundation you establish here.

Before we begin, on a scale of 0 to 10, how strongly do you rate your current ability to centre and ground yourself in any situation, and to connect deeply with what matters most to you?

(I recommend you record your answer to this and all the questions in this book, either in your own notebook, or in the large format paperback *Inner Leadership Workbook*, or in the electronic workbook which is available free from www.thechurning.net/p4913/.)

Step One: Centre

When I was 19 I took my youngest brother boating on a nearby pleasure lake. He was only six years old and as I rowed across the shallow water he became quite scared. I stopped and explained that because this was the first time he had ever been in a boat, the rocking was completely different from anything he had experienced before. But there was no real danger. The boat wasn't tipping over as he was afraid it might do. And even if it did, the water was very shallow and we could easily walk to shore, dry off, and start again. Once he got used to it, the rocking of the boat could even be fun!

These times of churning can often seem like this: the changes we face are very different from what we have been used to in the past, but usually there is no real danger. If there is danger, the later tools will show us how to identify that and what to do about it. But the first step, the first essential skill for leadership in times of change, is to be able to centre and ground at will. Then, as we shall learn by the end of the book, with a new attitude and new frameworks the churning can also become fun and enjoyable.

One time I remember as being particularly difficult for me to centre and ground was during my divorce. I found it very difficult to focus and work so I invented a simple technique: whenever I felt strong inner churning I would turn to focus on something else, perhaps looking out of the window at the people or the birds going about their day-to-day activities. This reminded me that, no matter how much churning I might be experiencing, it wasn't 'real': it was something I was creating in myself. That helped me to let go of those feelings and to deal with the situation as it really was. Many of the mindfulness approaches that are currently so popular are about creating this present-moment awareness.

Tool One:
Bring Yourself to Present-Moment Awareness

If you find yourself experiencing inner churning, simply catch yourself and bring yourself back to an awareness of what is happening in the present moment. Calm yourself and relax. Notice what is happening around you now. Describe it to yourself. Focus on your breath and slow it down. Take a deep breath and slowly release it. Then another. Notice what you are feeling in your body. How would you describe it? Where in your body are you feeling it? Ask yourself: is something external happening to me right now, or am I creating this churning for myself? Am I remembering something that happened in the past or imagining something that might happen in the future? Then shift your attention back to what is actually happening around you right now.

If your churning is coming from remembering the past or imagining the future, Chapter 2 will provide tools to make sense of that. For now, prepare yourself by centring: return to the present moment. Notice and name what you are thinking and feeling, and what is going on around you *now*, in this present moment.

(It is useful to record your answers in your workbook.)

The next two tools are more structured approaches for achieving the same thing: for letting go of churning and coming back to the present moment. They centre you so that you become ready to ground yourself and then move on to the tools of the later chapters, building step by step towards inspiration and joy.

I cannot know how relevant these tools will be for every reader right now. If you are currently feeling very calm and centred then these tools might not *seem* to add much value. But if you have recently experienced a highly traumatic event then these tools will to help you to re-centre before we move on to the rest of *Inner Leadership*. And for all of us, they provide an important starting point: a reliable baseline that we can return to at any time.

Like rowing in a boat for the first time, these tools might be different from what you have been used to in the past. But new challenges call for new solutions, so even if your life is calm right now I recommend you practice these tools so you know where they are when you need them, or when the people around you do. After all it is better to learn to swim before you get thrown in at the deep end.

Tool Two: The Sedona Method

Another technique for centring is called the Sedona Method. It involves paying close attention to what you are experiencing, and then asking yourself three simple questions.

To begin the technique, stop for a moment. You might be sitting down or standing up. Your eyes can be open or closed.

Now think about an issue that has been causing you to churn and that you would like to feel freer about. Focus inside your body. Notice where the churning appears and how it feels. Notice any thoughts that come with these feelings. Welcome them. Allow them to be.

Then ask yourself, is it possible that I could feel differently from the way I am feeling, just for a short time? Just for now, *could* I let these thoughts and feelings go?

Then ask, do I want to let them go? *Would* I let them go?

And the third question is, When?

This is the Sedona Method. Stop, think about the issue, notice what you are thinking and feeling, welcome those thoughts and feelings, and then ask yourself:

Can I drop them?

- Just for now, could I let these thoughts and feelings go?
- Would I?
- When?

What many people find at this point is that the level of churning they experience drops significantly.

You can then repeat the process as required. Notice the thoughts and feelings you now have. Accept them. Then ask yourself, "Just for now, could I let these thoughts and feelings go? Would I? When?"

The full Sedona method goes far beyond this and you can find out more at www.sedona.com.

In their book *The Problem is the Solution*, Marcella Weiner and Mark Simmons describe how to extend the technique and heighten your control, by first releasing any tensions, then intensifying them as much as you can, then flipping back and forth between the two.

But for our purposes these three questions of the Sedona Method are enough to let go of any inner churning and centre ourselves.

All we have to do is remember to use them.

Tool Three: Tapping or Emotional Freedom Technique

Another simple technique for centring ourselves is called Tapping or Emotional Freedom Technique (EFT). It releases negative emotions by tapping our fingers on various acupressure points around the body, in a way that is similar to the way acupuncture stimulates healing.

Frankly, the first time I came across this tool it seemed like a bunch of 'woo woo' bunk to me. But it works. Millions of people around the world have already benefited from Tapping and health professionals now use it routinely to address a wide range of symptoms, including releasing the anxiety of inner churning. Anecdotal evidence suggests that its use is becoming far more widespread: a new way of achieving the mindfulness we have recently become used to.

I don't understand how it works. But then I don't understand how my car, smartphone, tablet, or computer work either. And that doesn't stop me from using them.

If you are already feeling highly centred and want to skip ahead to the next section, please do. But if you are open to learning a new technique, or if you are experiencing any inner churning and want to release it, I fully recommend that you try this out. It's a best-in-class technique to add to your toolbox: a reliable way to become centred in even the most extreme circumstances.

To practice Tapping or EFT, first find a place where you can be undisturbed for a few minutes. Then focus on a feeling of churning you would like to release, perhaps something you've experienced during the past few days.

Notice where you are feeling it in your body and what it feels like. If you had to name it as an emotion, what would you call it? Notice that even though it is an emotional response to a situation, you still experience it as a physical sensation.

Now hold up one hand with the palm facing towards you. Gently start to tap the fleshy side of that hand (the karate chop point) with the fingertips of your other hand.

As you tap, say out loud three times, "Even though I have this feeling, I deeply and completely love and accept myself." This is called the setup.

Next we start to clear the blocked energy of your inner churning. Use your fingertips again to tap the top of your head seven times and as you do so say once, "This feeling."

Then, using only your first two fingers, tap between your eyebrows seven times and say, "This feeling."

Repeat this at the side of your eye, under your eye, and on your upper lip just under your nose, each time saying, "This feeling" and tapping seven times. Then do the same on your chin, the side of your collarbone, the side of your ribs, and then the inside of your wrist.

Now hold up your first hand again, but this time with the palm turned away from you. Using only your first finger tap the lower part of the thumbnail seven times and say, "This feeling."

Then tap the lower part of the nail of the first finger, middle finger, and then skip to your little finger, each time saying, "This feeling" and tapping seven times.

Now pause and focus on the sensations you were feeling. Have they reduced or gone away? Can you bring the feelings back?

If you want to repeat the process, start again from tapping the top of your head onwards, saying each time, "This feeling."

Mindfulness seemed strange and new a couple of years ago but has since entered the mainstream. The Sedona Method and Tapping now seem to be doing the same. They are proven techniques for enabling people who are churning to centre themselves.

Step Two: Ground

Having centred and restored our balance, the next step is to ground ourselves. This is about connecting strongly with who we are, what we care about, and how we choose to be in the world. Anchoring enables us to ground ourselves quickly at will.

Tool Four: Anchoring

Remember a time when you felt especially alive, in full flow, operating to the maximum of your potential and ability: a time that it would be useful for you to recall during stressful situations. It doesn't necessarily have to be a time when you were working. Choose an occasion when you felt most solidly grounded, composed, sure of who you are.

Write down what you remember about that time. Where were you? Who were you with? What were you doing? What were you working to achieve? Why? How did you feel? How was your body positioned? What was your posture? In particular, how were you holding your arms, back, and head? What did it feel like to be so grounded? Could you see, hear, taste, smell, or feel anything special?

Recreate the way your body was positioned then. Does that alter how grounded you feel now?

Do this for between one and three occasions. Focus on the most important aspects of each one. Look for the commonalities between your experiences. What is the essence of being grounded for you?

Now let's compare this with a standard position that many people find grounding. Stand with your feet shoulder width apart, knees slightly bent, and your back straight. Feel your weight passing down through your feet into the ground or floor. Imagine an invisible thread coming out of the top of your head, pulling your head and neck upwards. This is a very stable stance, solid, with a low centre of gravity.

Sway slightly from side to side or ask a friend to nudge you. Notice how you feel. Does this position feel more or less grounded than before? Shift between the stances and notice the differences.

Now let's compare these positions with the behaviour of someone you think of as being very grounded. Who is the most grounded person you can think of? Imagine that person in your role. How would they sit or stand? What would their posture be? How would they move? How would they speak? Copy them. Notice how you feel.

Compare this with the other positions and review the best of what you have learned and experienced. What position most strongly brings you a feeling of being grounded? Are there any images, smells, sounds, or tastes that are important to you? Shift into the position you have chosen, remember those images, smells, or sounds, and hold this for a few moments. Notice how you feel.

Now we want you to be able to recall this state at will.

It won't be possible to take on your preferred position in every situation, so we need to associate it with something else. This is called anchoring or creating an anchor.

One way to do this is to recall a key word, name, or image and associate that with the feeling of being grounded. Perhaps the words 'ground yourself', or 'Lincoln', or the image of an 'oak tree'. If this works for you, take some time now to choose such a word or image.

Another way is to create a physical anchor that can be activated by touching a particular part of your body. To create a physical anchor, first choose a part of your body (for example, your chin, your ear lobe, the second knuckle of the third finger of your left hand, and so on). Then touch that part of your body with another finger, thumb, or perhaps hold it between your thumb and forefinger. Bringing the two parts together is what forms the anchor.

Choose something that will look natural and inconspicuous in the situations where you intend to use it.

Now return to your feeling of being grounded and make that feeling as strong as you can. At the same time set up your chosen anchor. Hold the position, image, or thought while you focus on the feelings of groundedness. Then move out of position and relax. After a few moments return to your highly grounded state and initiate the anchor. Repeat until the anchor becomes associated with the feelings of groundedness. This might take a few days.

You now have techniques that enable you to centre and ground quickly and at will, returning to a state where you have felt especially alive and connected, in full flow, sure of who you are, and operating to the maximum of your ability and potential. The next step is to deepen that connection with yourself.

Step Three: Deepen Your Self-Knowledge

Learning to recover quickly from churning is all very well, but it is better not to experience that churning in the first place. Like a tree putting down deeper roots, deepening our groundedness and our connection with ourselves will make us less likely to be blown over. More importantly, it will also enable us to spread our leadership branches wider and grow into larger challenges and roles.

The relationship we have with ourselves is the only one that lasts our whole lifetime. It affects the quality of every other relationship we have, so it determines what we are able to achieve with others. It is our most important relationship.

The aim of this stage of the inner leadership journey is to deepen that connection with yourself and to build a strong foundation. The rest of the book will then build on that foundation, and you can always add to it with personal development courses and books of specific relevance for you. What is important here and now is to get into the habit of setting aside time for reflection: time to clear out any stress, recharge your batteries, focus on what is important to you, assess your progress, and build your capacity for taking the next right action.

As Elon Musk, CEO of Tesla Motors and SpaceX, says, "It's very important to have a feedback loop, where you're constantly thinking about what you've done and how you could be doing it better." The tools in this section provide three ways of achieving that.

Only you know what the quality of your relationship with yourself is now and how much of a priority it is for you to develop that. But of the three sections in this chapter, this is the most important. The more you apply and practise the lessons of this section, the more you will get out of the later chapters and they more they will then deepen your self-connection and -understanding still further. Time invested here will be repaid many times over.

Two thousand years ago the Romans knew that it was important to pray for *mens sana in corpore sano*: "a sound mind in a healthy body." Today the process of deepening our connection with ourselves also has two aspects, body and mind.

"Exercise is the single best thing you can do for your brain in terms of mood, memory, and learning," says John Ratey, psychiatrist at Harvard Medical School. "Even 10 minutes of activity changes your brain." Mind and body are one system and we hold snags from our mind in our body, so shifting the body is an effective way to shift and unblock the mind.

Hippocrates said, "Walking is our best medicine."

Richard Branson, founder of the Virgin Group of companies, says he gets four additional hours of productivity every day from a variety of workouts that include swimming, rock climbing, running, weightlifting, and yoga. Other leaders who emphasise the importance of daily exercise include US President Barack Obama and First Lady Michelle Obama, who both start the day with a workout. Anna

Wintour, editor-in-chief of American Vogue, begins her day with a tennis match.

When it comes to working on our minds Steve Jobs, co-founder and CEO of Apple, was well-known for practising Zen Buddhism. "Don't let the noise of others' opinions drown out your own inner voice," he said. Meditation connected him with that inner voice. Science has shown that meditation and other forms of mindfulness generate higher capacities to concentrate and to manage our emotions. Gandhi used its power to bring down an empire.

To centre and ground ourselves most deeply it makes sense to practise a combination of meditation and exercise. Author and businesswoman Ariana Huffington calls her early-morning yoga and meditation sessions 'joy triggers'. Walt Freese, former CEO of Ben & Jerry's and now the Sterling-Rice Group, starts and finishes each day with 15 minutes of meditation, exercises for at least an hour three days a week, and at weekends goes hiking, climbing, or skiing.

Part-way between exercise and meditation is creativity. In a world where everything is changing, the ability to innovate has become an increasingly important part of every leader's toolset. Innovation is applied creativity, so practicing your creativity will strengthen your creative 'muscle' and build your ability to innovate. Researcher Agnes Török says that making art is also her top recommendation for how to become happier and more resilient to the shocks that life throws at us. Engaging with the arts is a powerful way recharge your batteries.

Finally, all three of these can be combined with spending time in nature, which is another powerful way to reconnect with who we are and what matters most to us. Visits to hills or large bodies of water can be especially beneficial. In Japan the benefits of simply taking a short, leisurely visit to a forest, or 'forest bathing', are also widely known.

Only you will know the combination that is right for you now, and when to prioritise it into your schedule. If you don't currently spend time on these activities I suggest you start by committing at least five to 15 minutes a day and see where it leads you.

Tool Five: Physical Exercise

Since mind and body are one system, working on the body helps to strengthen the mind. Nietzsche wrote, "All truly great thoughts are conceived by walking."

Exercise makes us more aware of our bodies, which puts us more in touch with the inner wisdom of our gut feel and intuition.

Intense physical activity can also help to clear out the adrenaline associated with high levels of stress, and to process grief (see Chapter 7). Exercise can also be combined with spending time in nature.

What physical activity do you currently take? Do you enjoy it? Is it a priority for you do more or to take up a different form of exercise? When could you fit this into your schedule?

Remember that it only takes 10 minutes of daily activity to change your brain for the better.

Tool Six: Meditation, Mindfulness, and Reflection

For leaders focused on results, meditation might seem irrelevant. But Mahatma Gandhi used its power to bring down an empire. The story goes that one day, in the middle of intense negotiations, a journalist interviewed Gandhi and was surprised to discover that he meditated for an hour at the start of each day. This didn't make any sense to the journalist, who asked, "But what about when things are really busy and your workload is incredibly high?" "Well," replied Gandhi, "then I get up an hour earlier and I meditate for two hours."

The point is that meditation is not about relaxation. It is a way of getting things done. Abraham Lincoln famously said, "If I had eight hours to chop down a tree, I'd spend six hours sharpening my ax." Meditation sharpened Gandhi's inner axe. It brought him a degree of focus and clarity that enabled him to deal with his workload much more effectively.

One simple way to meditate is to sit quietly with your eyes closed, breathe slowly, and focus on your breathing. Count your breaths from one up to 10, then down again, and repeat. With your eyes still closed, look at the point between your eyebrows and focus your attention on the darkest area.

Not all forms of meditation involve sitting still with your eyes closed. Coming back to present-moment awareness is a simple way to meditate. The Morning Pages tool described in Chapter 2 can be a kind of meditation, and relaxing in a hot bath, going for a walk, or spending time in nature are three more. Time spent in nature can also be combined with many forms of exercise, perhaps in, on, or near hills, mountains, forests, or large bodies of water. Yoga, tai chi, and the martial arts combine meditation with movement. Mindfulness can be thought of as an entry-level form of meditation.

Another way to connect more deeply with yourself is to end each day with five to 15 minutes of reflection and appreciation for what has gone well, perhaps reviewing the lessons learned and your priorities for tomorrow. Then start each day with another five to 15 minutes remembering what went well yesterday and identifying what you want to achieve today.

Paradoxically, praising or thanking somebody else each day is also a simple way to achieve this deeper grounding. It also helps that person to become more grounded, and improves productivity and morale.

The important point here is to make time for reflection: time to (re)connect with yourself, your purpose, and your values. In a time of churning this is essential if you are not to be tossed around by every change that happens.

Beginning a daily practice now will create a habit that serves you well, both in facing the challenges and opportunities of life and in completing the exercises of the later chapters.

What forms of meditation, mindfulness, and reflection do you currently practice? Would it be beneficial for you to spend more time on this or to shift to a different form? When will you schedule this?

Tool Seven: Creativity

Is it important for you to develop your ability to innovate, to become more able to think outside the box? Would it be useful for you to find new ways to recharge your batteries?

What forms of creative expression do you currently take part in, whether creating your own work or engaging with the work of others? Is it a priority for you do more? What would happen if you did?

Do you feel drawn to spending time painting, drawing, cooking, discussing, debating, writing, reading, dancing, singing, sculpting, designing, collecting, arranging, making music, film, or something else?

Would you enjoy spending time watching, listening to, or otherwise enjoying the creative outputs of other people?

When will you schedule time for this?

Tool Eight:
Noticing Our Reflection in the Outside World

Another way to develop our connection with ourselves is to keep a list of quotations or aphorisms, key facts, art, or music that inspire us. Things that remind us what is true and important that we care about. Some of these might help us to centre and ground. Others might inspire us to take action.

You might find that certain key facts (perhaps about trends in your industry or the world at large) consistently make you feel angry or inspired, or provoke you into taking action. You might notice that there are certain principles that hold true for you, or values that you share.

Whatever these things are, start to make note of them as they come up. (You can use the workbooks to do this, or websites such as Pinterest and Evernote.)

Over time combine these notes, weed out what becomes less impactful, and keep whatever has the most meaning for you. Reword or reshape them if you want to.

In this way you will build a developing list of what you care about, what you believe in, and what you want to create instead.

This will be useful in the later chapters.

Conclusions

The purpose of this chapter has been to build a strong foundation that enables us to remain calm during times of change. When times are stable it will also enable us to extend and expand our leadership reach and influence.

We began with a set of tools intended to centre us even during extreme crisis. Present-moment awareness, the Sedona Method, and Tapping are simple techniques that are becoming more widespread. All we have to do is remember to apply them when we need them. Do you have a preference for one of these tools? How will you remind yourself to apply it when you are experiencing inner churning?

The second set of tools showed us how to return quickly to a highly grounded state, sure of who we are, and able to draw on the best of our ability and potential. Anchors not only enable us to return to this state at will but also to learn from other people we admire. What does your strongly grounded state feel like? What anchor will you use to retrieve it at will?

The third and most important section was about spending time getting to know ourselves better, deepening our grounded state. This involves setting aside time to remove stress, recharge our batteries, reflect, and build our capacity for taking the right action. Many leaders use exercise and meditation to accomplish this. We added creativity as a third approach. Spending time in nature can be combined with all three and is also important in its own right.

Maintaining a list of key quotes and other items that inspire you can act as a useful focus and will be helpful in the coming chapters.

Shakespeare said, "Unto thine own self be true, and it must follow as the night the day thou cans't not then be false to anyone." The solidity, inner knowledge, and self-confidence that comes from the activities described in this chapter will enable us to be true to ourselves in a wider range of circumstances. The rest of inner leadership will build on the foundation we lay down here.

Once you have learned to centre and ground sufficiently, and have begun an ongoing practice to deepen that grounding, it is time to move to Chapter 2 and make better sense of the situation you face.

Measurement

On a scale of 0 to 10, how strongly are you now able to centre and ground yourself in any situation, and deeply connect with what matters most to you? How does this compare with the start of the chapter?

What differences will this change make in your life? Professionally? Personally? What benefits will that bring? Financially? Emotionally? How valuable is that to you?

Is it a priority for you to strengthen these abilities further? Why? How much time will you allocate to achieving this?

(If you are using the workbooks you can record your answers there.)

Measuring Inner Leadership

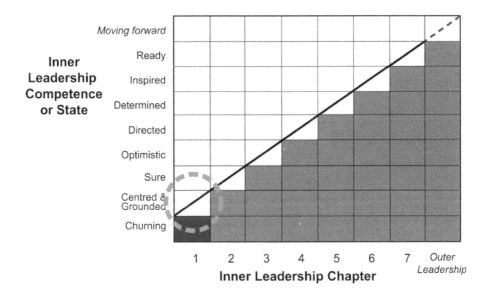

You might like to mark your improvement on the diagram.

How strong are your abilities at this first step of inner leadership? How does that compare with where you want to be or need to be with this competency?

2. MAKE SENSE OF THE SITUATION

Having centred and deeply grounded, the next step is to make sense of the situation we face.

This is important because in times of change it can be easy to misinterpret events. When the world is churning, the way things used to work is not necessarily a good guide to the way they work now, or to how they will work in the future. In addition, the reactions of stress, fear, and anxiety that change may bring can make it harder for us to see a clear way forward. At times like this it makes sense to pause and deliberately take stock of our situation.

The tools of *Outer Leadership* will show us how to do this from a strategic and operational point of view. But before we come to that, we first need to make sense from the point of view of our inner leader. We need to draw on the hidden power of our unconscious intuition and check for the mistaken assumptions and inappropriate emotional responses we might be making. Until we do this, any strategic or tactical assessment we might make is likely to be based on distorted interpretations and a limited range of options for moving forward.

This chapter provides two tools for avoiding these pitfalls.

The first is a structured approach for calling on the power of our intuition. When the world is changing, our conscious minds can easily become confused or misled. But our unconscious intuition will often be spotting patterns that our rational minds haven't yet seen. The first tool helps us to draw on that intuition, enabling us to make better sense of what is happening and identify new ways to move forward.

The second tool addresses the fact that the world no longer works the way it used to. This can lead to mistaken assumptions and inappropriate emotional responses. The second tool enables us to identify and unravel our distorted thinking to find other, better interpretations. It reminds us that, in a churning world, there is always more than one explanation, and more than one way events might turn out.

Both these tools will bring us increased clarity about the situation we face and more options for moving forward. This deepens the grounding we established in Chapter 1 and increases our chances of getting the results we want.

Before we begin, on a scale of 0 to 10, how do you rate your current ability to leverage the power of your unconscious intuition and to identify and make sense of your unconscious assumptions and emotional reactions? Make a note of the result.

Accessing the Power of
Our Unconscious Intuition

Our brains have evolved to notice movement and change because movement and change can mean one of three things: food, sex, or danger.

When so much of the world is changing at once, and our brains are trying to keep track of everything, it is easy for us to become overwhelmed. At this point we might shut down some of the information coming in or allow blind instinct to take over. But if we want to remain responsible leaders (of ourselves and others) it makes sense to look for more controlled responses before we reach that stage.

One solution is to try to analyse and interpret more data more quickly. Computers can do this for us but the result is often simply that we reach our own personal bottleneck again, this time with more data to consider about more items. Remember also that the information provided by computers is not reality: it is based on the assumptions and interpretations programmed into the computer by other (flawed) human beings. In a time of churning these beliefs may no longer hold true. The data in the computer may also be flawed. So although the information provided by computers can be useful, it is always at least one step removed from the real world we want to understand and act upon. And it doesn't fix the underlying blockage, which is our ability to make sense of what is happening.

Management requires data. Leadership requires something else.

Instead of trying to process infinite information about infinite possibilities, another approach is to expand our own bottleneck: to increase our ability to access and process information. Neuroscientists estimate that we are only conscious of about five percent of our cognitive activity – 95 percent is unconscious – so we can achieve this goal by learning to draw upon the power of our unconscious minds.

When sportspeople leap and stretch to put the ball exactly where they want it to go they are not using their conscious, rational minds. They are drawing on their intuition. When you suddenly remember something incredibly important that you thought you had forgotten, it is not your conscious, thinking mind that prompts you but your unconscious intuition. When tensions rise in a meeting because nobody can see a way forward, but then the perfect solution suddenly pops into someone's head, this is not our rational minds providing the answers: it is our intuition. When we stop 'thinking' we can achieve great things.

We all have this ability. Often it happens best in the moments of most extreme dynamic change, stress, and improvisation. Intuition is a muscle that can be trained. What we need is a way of accessing it reliably.

Tool One: Morning Pages

One way to access your intuition is to notice how your body reacts as you review the alternatives you are considering. Which does it seem to say 'yes' or 'no' to? Which inspire you and which depress you?

Another way is to toss a coin and see what answer you get. Then notice whether you then feel happy or disappointed with the result.

With practice, intuition can provide a shortcut to identifying the outcomes you want. (And you can still then think through whether those answers make sense and how you might achieve them.)

The exercises in the third section of Chapter 1 have already begun to develop this ability in you. But in her book, *The Artist's Way*, Julia Cameron described a more structured approach. She said she used the technique of Morning Pages to "provoke, clarify, comfort, cajole, prioritize, and synchronize the day at hand." We are going to use it as a tool for innovation: for spotting connections and uncovering patterns and solutions that we do not realise our unconscious minds have already seen. This will be useful for producing insights, resolving dilemmas, and for calming any anxieties we might have.

The tool can be used at any time of day but the best time to access your unconscious mind is first thing in the morning, before you are fully awake.

If you find that your logical mind is struggling to make sense of a situation, find ways to move forward, or simply isn't bringing you the answers you seek, try using this approach for enhanced lateral thinking. Allow the 95 percent of your brain that is unconscious to have a go. See what answers it comes up with. Then review those answers rationally before deciding how best to move forward.

The technique for Morning Pages is simply this:

> Sit down with pen and paper and write out longhand whatever comes into your mind. Continue until you have filled three sides of paper. Review what you have written. Make a note of the insights you uncovered. Then get on with the rest of your day. Repeat this the next morning, or for as long as you feel the need to draw on this extra source of information.

As you write the Morning Pages you will probably find your mind wandering. Follow it and see where it leads. You already spend most of your day analysing rationally so allow this time to try a different approach. Write down whatever comes into your mind without making sense of it and see what happens.

The first time you use this technique you probably won't magically resolve every issue you face but you will gain new insights.

In my experience, the first page is generally a jumble of thoughts as I settle into the process and find out where I am that day. The second page often throws up a couple of new ideas or whole avenues of thought I hadn't considered. And by the third page I may even be coming up with solutions.

I have noticed that these solutions are often related to thoughts I had on the first page (which seemed at the time to be irrelevant) so I have learned not to analyse or judge until the three pages are filled. Just follow the process and see where it leads.

The results won't always be terribly insightful. Some days you will simply get any niggling thoughts and worries out of your head and down on to the page. But that can be useful too: getting any issues down on paper enables your brain to relax, let go, and focus on your true priorities. It clears your mind and calms you, which extends the centring and grounding of Chapter 1. This resulting clarity may then produce further insights and reminders, or solutions you would never have thought of, options to consider.

Morning Pages are a way to produce insights, resolve dilemmas, or simply calm any anxieties you might have. Like all the tools in this book, you may find the technique unusual at first. But, if your usual approaches aren't bringing you the results you want, I recommend you give it a go. Many people adopt it as a daily routine.

As you use the Morning Pages over time you will likely find yourself able to access the intuitive parts of your brain more easily. You can then reserve using pen and paper for times when you want to make sense of a particularly tricky situation.

Unpacking Our Unconscious Thinking

The unconscious mind can be a powerful ally, but sometimes it makes mistakes. As Malcolm Gladwell explained in his bestselling book *Blink: The Power of Thinking Without Thinking*, we all make unconscious snap decisions. Sometimes we get them right. And sometimes we get them wrong.

In a time of change and churning the pressure to take these snap decisions increases. And so do the negative consequences of getting them wrong.

So, as well as using the Morning Pages to increase the times when we get it right, it also makes sense to use a tool for reducing the times when our unconscious decision-making gets it wrong.

In this section I will describe eight types of distorted thinking and biases we can all too easily unconsciously fall into, and then a tool for identifying and unscrambling them. This will enable us to make clearer sense of a changing world. It will also deepen the centring and grounding we began in Chapter 1.

Let's start with an example. It's an extreme case that is very unlikely to arise in our own lives but it clearly illustrates how three of the most common types of mistaken thinking can arise, as well as the negative outcomes that can follow when they do.

When Intuition Goes Wrong: An Extreme Example

Malcolm Gladwell's bestseller *Blink* tells the story of how four New York policemen mistakenly shot and killed Amadou Diallo. It is a tale of mistaken unconscious thinking that went very wrong indeed.

Driving past Diallo late at night, the officers sized him up and decided he looked suspicious. Backing up their patrol car they were amazed to find that he remained sitting on his doorstep. How brazen this man was, they thought, who didn't run at the sight of the police. They got out of their car and started walking towards him. Diallo reached into his pocket. In that blink of an eye the officers decided he was dangerous and opened fire, shooting him 19 times in seven seconds. It turned out he was reaching for his wallet.

Malcolm Gladwell tells this story as a way to illustrate how rapid, intuitive judgment can lead to disastrous results. It may not seem very relevant to our own lives – but the whole point about unconscious thinking is that we are not aware of it. In a time of churning it is useful to become more aware.

This story is also a stark reminder that in this time of churning our unconscious decisions can affect our own and other people's lives. Those impacts will likely be more difficult to predict and take longer to appear than in this example. But as responsible leaders we all have an obligation to ourselves, our families, and in some cases many thousands of people, to do our best to become aware of any mistaken unconscious thinking and then correct it. The tool below enables this.

There are eight main types of mistaken blink-of-an-eye thinking. Let's start by looking more closely at what happened in the Amadou Diallo case. That night there were three crucial unconscious decisions that the police officers unwittingly made.

Mis-blink 1: Value Judgments

The first mistaken blink-of-an-eye decision or 'mis-blink' that the police made as they drove past Diallo was that they decided he looked suspicious. They made a value judgment that classified him along a scale of 'good' to 'bad', and they placed him on the side of 'bad'.

This mis-blink shaped the direction of everything else that followed. It closed down one set of possible outcomes and made another set much more likely.

As leaders it is useful to keep our range of options open, especially when those options are changing and churning. When we judge a person as 'bad' or 'good' we unconsciously close down our range of possible responses to them and to the situation.

Judging a person as good is known as the halo effect and can have equally undesirable consequences. When we assume that a person who has positive qualities in one arena will be superior in other unrelated areas we are setting ourselves up to be disappointed. This is the kind of dynamic that con-artists rely on. It also leads to scandals around sex and corruption.

For clarity, I am not saying we should stop distinguishing between different levels of skill, experience, and capability. If I am hiring I still want to find the best candidate for the position. If I am having a medical operation or catching a plane I still want my surgeon and pilot to be qualified and skilful.

But there is a difference between what a person *does* and who a person *is*. There is a difference between saying "That supplier is useless" and "That supplier tends to be late with deliveries around the middle of the month so I wonder if we might be better off switching to another supplier or working with them to resolve the issue."

Being aware of this difference will keep us calmer, give us more options for action, and increase our likelihood of getting the results we want.

Mis-blink 2: Shoulds and Expectations

The police thought that Amadou Diallo should have run away as soon as he saw them. One officer even went so far as to say that he "was amazed" that Diallo did not run. This simple fact, that Amadou did not do what the police expected that he should do was a contributing factor to his death.

Should is a powerful word and if you want to avoid its hidden influence in your own life it is worth spending some time to become aware of its power. It is a word that strongly urges us to do things, but never quite explains why.

"You should do that" is clearly an instruction that you 'ought to', 'have to', or 'must' do a thing. It implies a duty, an obligation, or perhaps a correct way of doing things. But it doesn't explain *why* we ought to do the thing. For leaders this creates a problem.

"We should invest in that project," "She should do it this way," "He should have won the deal" – all of these give clear direction, but none explains why. Taking action on any of these statements is a step into the unknown. No matter who is saying it, the word 'should' is a red flag that an unconscious decision process is happening, perhaps even a deliberate manipulation.

In order to understand whether the recommended action will lead to an outcome we want, we need to ask: "Why?"

Sometimes we will get back what I call an 'output' answer: "Because then the outcome is likely to be X," or "Because this project brings the mix of risk and reward that we are looking for." Then if we need to we can always ask "Why?" again.

But if we get back an 'input' answer – "Because the policy is…," "Because the rules say…," or "Because that's what we always do…" – then we realise that this is just another set of 'shoulds'. Policy, rules, and habit are just a shortcut, a rule of thumb that reflects the way the world *used to* work. In a time of churning they might not reflect the way the world works now.

The way the world *should* be and the way the world *is* are two very different things, especially in a time of change. As leaders of ourselves and others it is important for us to understand this and to be clear about what we really mean.

Other meanings of the word 'should' include an estimate of probability ("The delivery should arrive by 11am."), an expression of astonishment ("You should have seen his face!"), and politeness or formality ("I should like to suggest…"). Should can also imply hindsight, as in, "I/You/We/They should have known better." Some of these instances may safely be ignored. But for others it is worth unpacking, "Why?"

We might end up choosing to take the same action we originally thought we should. But until we are clear what that really means, following any 'should' is little better than guessing.

Notice also that "thinking outside the box" really means "thinking outside our 'shoulds'." In a time of change this can be a useful way to find innovative solutions, such as Uber, Airbnb, Spotify.

How Should You Go to Market?

A man and his son were walking their donkey to market. Along the way they passed through a number of villages.

At the first village the people laughed at them. "You are so stupid," they said. "One of you should ride the donkey." That seemed like a good idea, so the son got on the donkey.

Then they came to the second village. "How terrible," the villagers said, "forcing an old man to walk while the young man takes it easy. The old man should ride." So the father and son swapped places.

At the next village they again found themselves the object of ridicule. "Idiots!" the people said. "You should both ride the donkey!" So they both got on the donkey.

And at the next village the people threw stones. "You should be ashamed of yourselves! Poor animal!" they cried. "You should be carrying the donkey, not the other way around."

You can probably see how this is going to turn out. At the next village the people told them they should stop carrying the donkey and simply walk to market. So they did.

Different people will always tell you different 'shoulds', and you will never be able to make them all happy. Inner leadership is about knowing what *your* own priorities are and why they matter to you. Knowing them and sticking to them will save you wasted time and energy in discussions and will get you to market faster, the way you want, without a sore back.

Chapters 1, 4, and 5 will develop this clarity for you. For now, letting go of 'shoulds' (and other mis-blinks) is a first step towards achieving that.

Mis-blink 3: Making Assumptions or Jumping to Conclusions

The third mistaken blink-of-an-eye decision made by the police officers happened when Amadou Diallo put his hand into his pocket. They assumed or jumped to the conclusion that he was reaching for a weapon.

We all make assumptions every day. We assume that when we pour coffee into a cup the cup will not dissolve or melt. We assume that if we set off by a certain time we will arrive by the time we need to. We assume that if we behave in a certain way towards our customers, co-workers, family, and friends then they will behave in a certain way back. But it doesn't always turn out that way.

In a time of change, past performance may not be indicative of future results. The more we can be aware of the assumptions we are making, the better we can identify alternative possibilities, and either make contingency plans or take different actions accordingly.

In Amadou Diallo's case there were two lots of assumptions going on, for both parties. One was about the attitude of the other person or people. The other was about how the future would turn out. Tragically, the police were assuming that Diallo was feeling aggressive towards them and would try to harm them, while Amadou Diallo was (apparently) assuming that the police had benevolent intentions towards him and that everything would turn out fine.

As leaders, our role is not to make assumptions. Neither is it to try to control everything (which is impossible anyway during a time of change). As leaders our role is to define and create the conditions for success as best we can: recognising what is in our control and what is not, then mapping out what might happen and assigning our limited resources accordingly.

The tool below will help us to achieve this, by showing how to identify the assumptions and other mis-blinks we might be making, and then asking what alternative interpretations or explanations might also be possible.

Before I describe the tool, let's first list the eight main types of mis-blink that people often make.

Eight Common Mis-blinks

Mis-blinks are ways in which people can confuse their own thinking, making unconscious snap decisions without realising they are doing so. We all do this from time to time, and in a time of change it becomes much more likely. By becoming aware of our mis-blinks we can learn to spot them and so avoid the unwanted consequences they bring.

The eight common types of mis-blink are:
1. Value judgments
2. Shoulds and expectations
3. Making assumptions or jumping to conclusions

4. Attachment to outcome
5. Dependency
6. Blinkered or extreme thinking
7. Mistaking feelings for truth
8. Blaming and scapegoating

Let's briefly review each of these unconscious biases, starting with a quick summary of the first three. Then we will examine a tool for unscrambling these mis-blinks and finding alternative interpretations.

The box on pages 34-35 provides some examples.

1. Value Judgments

This mis-blink happens when we equate a person with their successes or imperfections, and then label them either as 'good' or 'bad'. We lump together who they are with what they did, taking a quality that applied in one situation and assuming that it applies to the whole person. But there is a difference between who a person *is* and what a person *does*.

This mis-blink can apply equally to positive qualities (the halo effect) as to negative ones. And we can mistakenly apply it just as much to ourselves as we do to other people.

The reality is that we all have a mix of strengths and weaknesses. We can all make a contribution in some areas and are best avoiding others.

A story from ancient China illustrates how qualities and behaviours that we consider 'bad' in one situation can become 'good' in another. A city came under attack from a superior army and for many months the people suffered. Then a notorious burglar and thief, locked up in jail, offered to help. That night he crept unseen into the enemy's camp and left a dagger in the sleeping general's tent. The general doubled the guard but on the second night the thief crept in again and left a dagger on the sleeping general's pillow. The next morning the enemy general gathered his troops and departed because he knew that on the third night the dagger would be left in him.

When situations change, what was 'bad' can become 'good' and vice versa. In a time of change, both judgments become unreliable.

Judgment words come pre-packed into much of our everyday language, for example: strength, weakness, opportunity, threat. These words pre-judge what the situation represents and close down our range of options for responding to it. (We will return to this in Chapter 3.)

2. Shoulds and Expectations

Whenever we expect that something should or should not happen in a certain way it is a sign that unconscious thinking is happening: an old rule of thumb that may no longer apply.

In a time of churning it makes sense to check whether we still agree with that unconscious thinking, by asking "Why?"

If the 'should' is about the future ("I, You, We, or They should do such and such…") then keep asking why until you have truly understood how the proposed action will bring about a particular outcome, and why that is better than the alternatives.

If the 'should' is about the past ("I, You, We, or They should have done such and such…") then ask yourself whether that is realistic or just wishful thinking based on hindsight. Keep asking why until you have uncovered what specific action done differently in the past might have led to the outcome you wanted. Then learn that for the future.

Alternatively, if the 'should' turns out to be a desire for unrealistic perfectionism, remember that the way the world is and the way it should be are two different things. The question is, which parts are we willing to accept and which parts are we willing to apply the time, energy, and resources to change?

We can apply this 'should' mis-blink to ourselves just as much as to other people and situations. All are equally inappropriate.

3. Making Assumptions or Jumping to Conclusions

This mis-blink happens when we assume that people are reacting favourably or unfavourably towards us, based on minimal evidence, or when we arbitrarily expect or predict that things will turn out in a particular way. How do we know what their intentions are? How likely is it that things will go the way we expect? What else is possible?

The problem here is not whether we eventually turn out to be right or wrong. The problem arises when we allow our assumptions to restrict the range of actions we consider.

If we spot ourselves making assumptions or jumping to conclusions, the key questions to ask ourselves are:
- How much evidence is there for our interpretation?
- What would be the consequence if we were mistaken (or correct)?
- What other possibilities are there?
- How likely is each one?

4. Attachment to Outcome

As leaders we are naturally focused on creating results. Having a strong emotional attachment to doing so can help us to achieve them.

But in a time of churning no outcome is ever guaranteed. Having a strong emotional attachment to a goal we do not reach is likely to bring about feelings of failure (a value judgment) and lower productivity, together with difficulty in then moving on.

In a time of churning, it therefore becomes useful to let go of our emotional attachment to the outcomes we seek, while at the same time retaining our absolute intention to achieve them. It becomes useful, like Thomas Edison, to be able to say, "I have not failed, I've just found 10,000 ways that won't work." Then press on with our next attempt.

The way to accomplish this is by keeping an eye on the big picture and knowing our ultimate objectives. Then, if the tactical situation changes, we can find a new goal that achieves our desired outcomes and aligns better with the way reality has turned out.

I remember a leadership development training exercise at a B2B company I used to work in. High potential leaders took part in a role-play to test how quickly they could sell a particular deal to a customer and what terms they could negotiate. After a few minutes the customer would subtly start to indicate that she was no longer interested in the old deal but now wanted to buy something else. The real test was to see how quickly the young leaders would let go of their attachment to selling the original deal and focus instead on what the customer now wanted to buy.

Knowing your wider purpose will help you to let go of your emotional attachment to any particular goal or outcome because, as author, salesman, and motivational speaker Zig Ziglar put it, "When obstacles arise you change your direction to achieve your goal, you do not change your decision to get there."

5. Dependency

Dependency is a constraint we sometimes place upon ourselves when we know what we want to do, but refuse to do it unless another person behaves in a particular way. We make our own preferred behaviour conditional or 'dependent' on the behaviour of another.

In many cases this is a healthy part of normal business: "I will deliver this service if you pay me XYZ amount" or "I will pay you XYZ amount if you deliver this service." But in other contexts dependency can cut us off from our true inner leader and prevent us from achieving goals that are important to us.

In June 2014, for example, Tesla Motors decided to open up the patents for its batteries. It gave up the royalties and licensing fees that it would have been paid under normal business practice because it realised that these were holding the company back from achieving its strategic goals.

As founder Elon Musk wrote in his blog:

"Yesterday, there was a wall of Tesla patents in the lobby of our Palo Alto headquarters. That is no longer the case. They have been removed, in the spirit of the open source movement, for the advancement of electric vehicle technology.

Tesla Motors was created to accelerate the advent of sustainable transport. If we clear a path to the creation of compelling electric vehicles, but then lay intellectual property landmines behind us to inhibit others, we are acting in a manner contrary to that goal. Tesla will not initiate patent lawsuits against anyone who, in good faith, wants to use our technology."

In giving up the patents, Tesla let go of its 'dependency' to only share battery information if others paid it a licence fee. It freed itself to behave as the leader it truly is.

Dependency can be a tricky mis-blink to spot since it combines an attachment (to a low-level outcome) with a should (pay patent licence fees). But in a time of churning the old rules ('shoulds' and attachments) break down, so letting go of a dependency is a key step that can allow new business models to emerge. Look, for example, at what happened when Uber and Airbnb let go of their requirement or dependency to own or directly control their own taxis, hotels, and employees.

When we constrain our behaviour to depend on the actions of another person we effectively cut ourselves off from achieving the results we most value. We also cut ourselves off from achieving our full potential and identity as a human being.

Think of any leader you admire and I guarantee that at some point in their lives they chose to do what they felt was right, irrespective of whether anybody else agreed, approved, or reciprocated. Sometimes it is necessary to do what is right for you simply because it is the right thing for you to do.

This is what Elon Musk has done.

6. Blinkered or Extreme Thinking

This mis-blink arises when a person focuses only on the undesirable aspects of a situation and ignores the favourable ones. Or they might see only the positive elements, insisting somehow that the negative aspects don't count.

Alternatively, a person might blow tiny elements of a situation out of all proportion, making mountains out of molehills. Or they might block out or ignore a key factor, the well-known elephant in the room that no-one talks about.

All these are indicators that the unconscious mis-blink known as blinkered thinking or extreme thinking might be happening: a reaction that leads us to see the world in terms of extremes or polar opposites: black or white, good or bad, all or nothing, utter failure or success beyond our wildest dreams.

Other words that indicate the likely presence of blinkered thinking include everyone/no-one, everything/nothing, everywhere/nowhere, always/never, impossible/inevitable, and all/every/none.

When we describe the world in these extreme terms we not only disempower ourselves from taking action to change the future, we also forget that this mis-blink is a misinterpretation *we* are making, and that therefore *we* have the power to change.

Because this type of blinkered thinking describes extremes it can be relatively easy to spot. But the fact that it contains extreme viewpoints can also make it difficult to change once we get caught up in it. (See also Mis-blink 7, Mistaking feelings for reality, and Mis-blink 4, Attachment to outcome.)

If you identify this kind of thinking in yourself or others, first realise that it is a mis-blink, not reality. Then identify which extreme the person is getting caught up in and what would be the opposite of that. Then ask what possibilities lie between the two extremes and how likely they each are. The Morning Pages tool may be useful here.

In a churning world, nothing is ever impossible or guaranteed. The best we can do is to set a clear intention and then work to create conditions where our desired outcome is most likely to occur.

7. Mistaking Feelings for Truth

This type of mis-blink occurs when we take our feelings as being true, irrespective of the evidence. It is a circular train of thought that amplifies the effects of the other mis-blinks by saying, "Because I feel this [mis-blink] so strongly, it must be true, which makes me feel worse, which means [the mis-blink] must be truer…"

Equally, mistaking feelings for truth can lead to overconfidence and under preparation: "Because I am feeling good, I am bound to succeed; therefore I don't need to prepare."

Human beings are emotional creatures. Emotions are what make our lives worth living. Without them there would be no joy, no love, no sports, no art, no movies, no theatre, no dance, no comedy, no music, no friends, no lovers. Emotions are what make us more than just machines, so the problem is not the feelings themselves but the way that we *interpret* them and the actions we then take as a result.

Mistaking feelings for truth becomes a problem when we forget to look for supporting evidence for our feelings, and when we forget that no matter what the situation is we can always choose how we respond.

8. Blaming and Scapegoating

When a situation turns out differently from the way we wanted and we then blame an individual (or ourselves) for something that the person had only partial control over, we are mixing up the person, the event, and our feelings about the event. We are scapegoating the individual.

Human beings have used this way of getting rid of unpleasant feelings for thousands of years, but it is inappropriate and it doesn't solve the problem.

This complex mis-blink reaction is likely to contain a mixture of a value judgment (of the person), attachment (to the outcome that didn't happen), blinkered thinking (that the failure to get the outcome we wanted is somehow a complete disaster), expectation (that it should have turned out differently from the way it did), assumption (that it was going to), mistaking feelings (our judgment of the person) for truth (that the person is to blame), and perhaps even dependency (for the actions that we ourselves didn't take that might have created a different outcome).

Scapegoating and blame are great ways to project a whole range of our emotions on to another person. But, like the arch-villain in a movie who kills any team member who fails to meet their objectives, scapegoating an individual will only make our organisation weaker and discourage others from attempting to create the future innovations that these times of change will need. It really doesn't help.

Better instead to use the tools of Chapter 1 to centre and ground ourselves and those around us. Then use the tool below to analyse our thinking and learn from what happened. Work out what we might do differently next time, and what we will do now to move forward.

Tool Two: Resolving Our Mis-blinks

In a churning world, the likelihood that we will mislead ourselves with these kinds of unconscious misinterpretations rises dramatically. And so does the risk of negative consequences if we do so.

We are now ready to use the second tool of this chapter, to find out whether we are distorting our thinking with any of these eight mis-blinks. You can use this tool if you are finding yourself feeling inexplicably frustrated about something over an extended period of time or to gain clarity over any situation that is making you churn.

Working in competitor analysis and strategic process improvement taught me that one of the best ways to achieve new outcomes is by benchmarking: looking for existing best practices in other industries and adapting them to your own needs. The following tool is adapted from David Burns' excellent cognitive behavioural therapy approach.

Examples of Mis-blinks

A wise person once said, "Don't believe everything you think."
The eight mis-blinks provide a quick way to spot when we might
be thinking something that isn't true.

As examples, imagine what a senior manager at Sony might
have thought in 2011, when floods in Thailand suddenly turned a
global profit forecast of $0.8bn into a $1.2bn loss. Here are some
of those imagined mis-blinks, together with examples of what
more realistic thoughts might have been. You can probably think
of others.

The tool in the next section provides a structured approach
for identifying your own mis-blinks and coming up with
alternative interpretations that may be more realistic.

1. Value Judgments

"The company will make a loss this year. I am a bad leader."

Possible realistic thought: "Yes, the firm will make a loss, but it
would have been even larger if I had not taken actions A, B, and
C earlier in the year."

2. Shoulds and Expectations

"I should have known the floods would happen and taken steps
to prepare for them."

Possible realistic thought: "Nobody expected so much rain.
Effective flood defences would have cost almost as much as the
clean-up, and might never have been needed."

3. Making Assumptions, Jumping to Conclusions

"The board of directors will fire me."

Possible realistic thought: "That is possible but unlikely. If they
do then I will be able to handle it because…"

4. Attachment to Outcome

"I loved this job. I wanted to stay here until retirement. I will
never get another job like this."

Possible realistic thought: "I have never stayed in one role longer than five years. I have a good track record. I know of several other potential roles…"

5. Dependency
"I will resign if [Person X] does not apologise for what he said to me on the phone."

Possible realistic thought: "[Person X] was reacting in the heat of the moment. He can't see his own mis-blinks. That is his issue. Quitting a job I love over that would be ridiculous. I am clearly feeling upset. I need to centre and ground, then make clear sense of the situation…"

6. Blinkered or Extreme Thinking
"Bad luck always happens to me."

Possible realistic thought: "The floods affected nearly all the firms in the area. We were lucky not to be hit as badly as Z."

7. Mistaking Feelings for Truth
"I feel so upset about this situation, I must be a bad leader."

Possible realistic thought: "I am feeling upset because I care about our financial performance, our people, and the local community. They are part of my values. If I use these feelings to help identify priorities for action then we can use the way we respond to this crisis as an opportunity to strengthen relationships with our people and the community, and so improve results in the future. There will always be crises. It is how we respond to them that matters."

8. Blaming and Scapegoating
"I will fire the Facilities Manager. It is all her fault."

Possible realistic thought: "We all knew there was a risk but none of us did anything about it. If the Facilities Manager had asked for money for flood defences I would have said no."

The tool starts by depersonalising the situation, making it less personally charged, more objective. Then it helps us to find alternative interpretations and decide how likely they are. The result is that we not only realise where we might be misleading ourselves with mis-blinks, but also form new, more realistic interpretations.

Even if we decide to stick with our original interpretation, this tool gives us a structured approach for managing the uncertainty and ambiguity of this time of churning. No matter what the situation, it brings us a clearer, more nuanced, and more grounded understanding of what is going on. This reduces risk by reminding us that there is never only one explanation for a situation, nor only one way in which it might turn out. It also provides a more balanced, grounded starting point from which to look for alternative ways forward.

Applying the tool also brings us direct personal experience of the fact that it is not *what happens* that affects us emotionally but the way that we *interpret what happens*: the meanings *we create* about what we *think* an event means. Finding new interpretations releases the inner churning and uncertainty of our mis-blinks. This brings us another step closer to the joy and inspiration that inner leadership is all about.

To apply this tool, first think of a situation that has been triggering you emotionally, making you churn, or that you are simply stuck on. Then follow these nine steps.

1. First, take a piece of paper, turn it widthways, and write across the top a short factual description of the situation or what has happened. In the examples above this might be "Our factory has flooded" or "Person X shouted at me on the phone." Another example situation might be "I have been appointed to breathe new life into Product Z."

2. Draw a line across the page under your description and add five columns. (Alternatively use the table in the workbooks.)

3. In the first column write your interpretations of the event. What does it mean? What are the implications? What, especially, does it mean about *you*? Write down, in brief, all the thoughts that you have about the situation.
   (In the examples box above, these unconscious interpretations include "I am a bad manager," "I should have prepared flood defences," "I will never find another job," and so on. For the

product development example, apparently positive mis-blink thoughts might include "I am a genius. Sales will double within a year. There's no need for any market testing. I should demand to manage Product Y as well," and so on.)

4. In the second column, on a scale of 0 to 10, write how sure you are that each thought or interpretation is correct. How likely is each one to be true? What is the evidence for each statement?

5. Now compare the first of your interpretations (column 1) with the eight common mis-blinks. Does your interpretation include any mis-blinks? If it does, write their names or numbers in the third column.
   If you are unsure, write down any that *might* apply. The more you include, the greater your chances of finding alternative viewpoints and explanations.

6. For each of these potential mis-blinks, use the descriptions above to identify alternative explanations that might also be true. (In the examples box, these are the 'realistic thoughts'.) Write these in the fourth column.

7. In the fifth column, again on a scale of 0 to 10, write how likely you think each of the new interpretations or 'realistic thoughts' is. How true do you think they are?

8. Repeat steps 5, 6, and 7 for all the thoughts and interpretations you listed in the first column.

9. Look again at the thoughts and interpretations you wrote in the first column. Compare them with the new interpretations you now have in column 4. How likely do you now think your original interpretations are? Add this to column 2.

By this stage you will likely have a new understanding of your situation. You will have seen that there are other ways of interpreting what has happened and that your original understanding is not quite as certain as it once seemed. You are likely to feel more positive, less constrained, and you have a wider scope for taking action. This what we will look at more closely in the next chapter.

Conclusions

When the world is churning and things no longer work the way they used to, the second step of inner leadership is to pause and make sense of the situation. If you have experienced any churning while reading this chapter, remember to use the tools of Chapter 1 to centre and ground.

The first tool in this chapter has brought us a structured approach for calling on the power of our unconscious intuition. Morning Pages are a reliable way to spot patterns that our rational minds may have overlooked, and to calm anxieties, resolve dilemmas, and produce new insights.

The second tool has provided a way to identify the mistaken assumptions and interpretations that become more likely in a time of change, and to generate alternative explanations and insights. Uncovering our mis-blinks in this way brings us a more balanced view. It reminds us that there is never only one explanation or only one way things might turn out. And it gives a structured approach for managing this ambiguity. Applying this second tool also provides experiential learning of the fact that it is the way that we *interpret* a situation that creates the feelings we have about it.

Both these tools deepen the grounding of Chapter 1.

The bottom line of this chapter is that suppliers may go bust, customers may switch to competitors, and new technologies may threaten our existing business models, but none of these events need be the end of the world. They simply mean that things have not turned out the way we expected (surely not a surprise in a time of change) and we will have to take a different route to get to where we want to be. As long as we are clear on where we are now and where we want to get to, all we need to do is plot a new way forward.

Chapters 1 and 2 have been about getting clear on where we are now. Chapters 4 to 6 will be about defining where we want to get to. Having made sense of the situation, it is now time to identify our alternative ways forward. This is what we shall do in Chapter 3.

Measurement

On a scale of 0 to 10, how able are you now to leverage the power of your unconscious intuition and to identify and make sense of your unconscious and emotional reactions? How does this compare with where you were at the start of the chapter?

What differences will this make in your life? Professionally? Personally? What benefits will that bring? Financially? Emotionally? How valuable is that to you?

Is it a priority for you to strengthen these abilities still further? Why? How much time will you allocate to achieving this?

(Record your answers in whatever workbook or notebook you are using.)

Measuring Inner Leadership

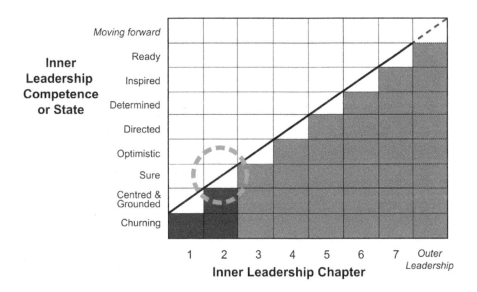

3. FIND MORE OPPORTUNITIES

Having centred, grounded, and made sense of the situation, the next step is to decide how to move forward. Before we can do that, we first need to identify alternatives.

In a time of change, the obvious ways forward may no longer be the best. New opportunities will be emerging all the time, so it makes sense to pause explicitly and look for them. The tools of *Outer Leadership* will enable us to do this from a strategic and operational point of view. But before we come to that, this chapter is first about looking for alternative ways forward, based on the inspiration that lies at the very heart of inner leadership.

Success will always be a combination of the quality of our plan and the enthusiasm with which we implement it. History is filled with examples of people who beat the odds simply because they felt more inspired. So, in a time of change, when all ways forward will be difficult and unpredictable, it makes sense to look first not for what we think is possible but for what will bring the greatest inspiration to our customers, investors, employees, and ourselves. It makes sense to look first for what will most inspire us, then for how to achieve that.

Having understood the situation, this chapter is about shifting our focus away from "How shall we respond?" to the more proactive, "What do we most want to create?" In a time of change, this is what will sustain us. And the way we find it is not by strategising ever more deeply based on the way the world *used to* work but by finding new inspiration for the way the world *could be.*

This chapter is about innovation and ideation. It is about learning to look past the issues we face to find the opportunities to create whatever we most desire. Then we can work out how to make them happen. And then choose the combination of inspiration and implementation that works best for us.

The chapter begins by discussing what we mean by an opportunity and a threat. It gives some examples and describes the benefits that come simply from *looking for* opportunities. It then reveals the ten types of opportunity that exist in any situation and provides tools for finding them. The chapter closes by asking you to identify the ten types of opportunity to create inspiration that exist in the situation you face today. (Then, in the next chapter, you will choose between them.)

Before we begin, on a scale of 0 to 10, how strongly do you rate your current ability to find the opportunities in a crisis?

Rethinking Opportunities and Threats

When I was fairly fresh out of business school I was asked to prepare a strategic business plan for a half billion dollar pan-European technology services business.

The sector was undergoing a lot of change, both in the technologies being used and the way these were being delivered. The needs of the customer and the customer's customers were also changing. So I thought it made sense to analyse the situation using the well-known SWOT analysis tool we had been taught on the MBA: to identify the internal Strengths and Weakness of the business and compare these against the external Opportunities and Threats in the marketplace.

The trouble was, the model didn't make sense. Or rather, it just wasn't useful. The shift from old technology (mainframe computers) to new technology (client-server) was a threat to the existing business model. But if we moved fast to adopt the new technology then it could also become an opportunity to upgrade old systems. The rise of cheaper remote programming centres that competitors were building in Ireland (and later India) was a threat if we did nothing. But if we built our own data centres then it became an opportunity. The strengths we thought we had in delivering old technologies were fast becoming an irrelevant weakness. And as the needs of our customers and their customers changed, so the ability to deliver what they wanted yesterday became a ball and chain that held us back from delivering what they would want tomorrow.

What I discovered then was that threats and opportunities don't really exist. Yes, there are changes in the marketplace, but whether those changes turn out to be beneficial or disadvantageous depends more on how we respond to them than on any intrinsic characteristic of the situation. Labelling them as 'opportunities' or 'threats' is a mis-blink that pre-judges both the situation and the outcome, and closes down our available responses.

The same applies to 'strengths' and 'weaknesses': a shifting marketplace alters the relative priorities of different capabilities. Physical presence, for example, might become more important than low cost, or vice-versa. The ability to manage relationships (and the commitment to deliver whatever is needed no matter what the future holds) might become more important than strengths in any one particular area. But even the solidity of a long-established relationship can become a weakness if the seductive promises of a new entrant outweigh the well-worn familiarity of the incumbent. Even zero capability can become a strength if it allows us to build quickly from scratch what the market needs now, leapfrogging the outdated delivery methods that others are stuck with. What seem to be strengths can become weaknesses and vice-versa.

When the world is churning there are, paradoxically, no inherent strengths, weaknesses, opportunities, or threats. There is only our ability or inability to deliver what is needed today and tomorrow. Yes, we have capabilities, competencies, and resources. But whether these are useful or not-useful depends not on what they are, or even on how the marketplace changes, but on the choices we make about how to combine the two and move forward. Even what seems like an absolute, unequivocal threat can be beneficial if it spurs us to greater action.

This realisation that the future is unpredictable can make people's emotions churn even more. We like the idea of certainty, predictability, control. When we don't know how things are going to turn out it can seem as if the top priority is to quickly make a plan, any plan, just so we can imagine we know what is going to happen and make our inner churning go away. But in a time of churning this knee-jerk reaction no longer serves us. When change is all around, what drives success is our ability to develop an opportunity mindset, to pause and spot the new opportunities that are emerging, then map a path to reach them; to live like Doctor Who and turn each crisis into an adventure.

What this section shows is that opportunities do not exist separately 'outside' us. They exist as the result of the *choices we make* about how to combine external events with our inner abilities – and then the levels of inspiration we are able to generate to pursue them.

When everything is changing, opportunities are what we choose them to be, based on what most *inspires* us and how much we are able to inspire others to agree.

Learning to find that inspiration and spot these opportunities is what this chapter is all about.

The Parable of the Taoist Farmer

There was once a farmer in ancient China who owned a horse. "You are so lucky!" his neighbours told him, "to have a horse to pull the cart for you." "Maybe," the farmer replied.

One day he didn't latch the gate properly and the horse ran away. "That is terrible news!" his neighbours cried. "Such bad luck!" "Maybe," the farmer replied.

A few days later the horse returned, bringing six wild horses with it. "How fantastic! You are so lucky," his neighbours told him. "Maybe," the farmer replied.

The following week the farmer's son was breaking-in one of the wild horses when it threw him to the ground, breaking his leg. "Oh no!" the neighbours cried. "Such bad luck, all over again!" "Maybe," the farmer replied.

The next day soldiers came and took away all the young men to fight in the army. The farmer's son was left behind. "You are so lucky!" his neighbours cried. "Maybe," the farmer replied.

The Problem Is the Opportunity

So, there are no such things as strengths or weaknesses, nor opportunities and threats. There is only how we choose to respond to the situations we find ourselves in.

Here are some examples of apparent problems that turned out to be opportunities:

- The high-speed train tunnel beneath a Japanese mountain that had a 'problem' with flooding, until they realised that the water, filtered by the mountain, was very pure and could be collected, bottled, and sold as mineral water
- The 'problem' of burrs catching on clothing, which led to the invention of Velcro
- The 'problem' of the failed petri dish experiment in which bacteria wouldn't grow, which turned into an opportunity when Alexander Fleming discovered it contained penicillin
- The tent salesman who went to California during the gold rush, only to find that the weather was so warm the miners didn't need tents – so he cut up his stock and turned it into Levi Strauss jeans instead
- The 'problem' of fresh food that rotted, providing the spur to the invention of refrigeration

These cases are all different, but they all share one thing in common. In all of them, the core difference between these leaders and every other person who has found themselves in a similar situation (but responded differently) was their inner attitude of mind: the choice to see the situation not as a 'problem' but as an 'opportunity'.

This intention to spot the opportunities in difficult situations, to find inspiration where others see only threats, is *the* attitude that defines inner leadership.

We can train ourselves to recreate it by realising that all these people could simply have fixed the problems they faced: by draining the water from the tunnel, wearing different clothes, washing out the petri dishes, taking the tents somewhere rainy, or throwing the rotten food away. Instead something else happened.

We will never know quite what it was, but it must have been one of three things:

1. Chance, Synchronicity, or Serendipity
    Levi Strauss might have been sitting on his stack of tents, crying at the unfairness of fate, when a miner with ripped trousers walked by and Strauss realised his hard-wearing fabric would make good jeans.

2. Intuition
    The inventor of the sewing machine reputedly solved the problem of how to make the needle work in a dream. James Cameron had the ideas for Terminator and Avatar in the same way, as did Stephenie Meyer, creator of the successful Twilight series of books and films.

3. Seeing the Problem as an Opportunity
    Reframing the nature of the problem, and then asking where, how, or for whom it might be an opportunity.

Here are three simple ways in which we can increase our own abilities to achieve these things. They do not guarantee that we will find a world-changing solution every time, but they do make us more likely to make the best of whatever situations arise.

Tool One: Daily Appreciation for Serendipity

The first approach is to develop our serendipity. Serendipity is a word that has come to mean a 'lucky accident' that miraculously shows us the solution. But when Horace Walpole originally coined the term in 1754 he also saw serendipity as the *quality of mind* that allows us to spot solutions when the 'lucky accident' occurs. "Serendipity is a quality of mind, which through awareness, sagacity, and good fortune allows one frequently to discover valuable things while seeking something else."

We can increase our chances of experiencing this quality of mind by changing the way we view the world. Towards the end of each day, take the time to identify three to five things that went well for you that day, and for which you are grateful. I set a reminder on my phone. Writing down the items will help you to embed the process initially. After a while you will find it takes no time at all.

Actively praising or complimenting somebody each day also gets us into the habit of spotting not just the problems but what is going well. This also builds morale. The Chapter 1 activities for developing creativity will also develop your ability to spot solutions.

These practices get us into the habit of seeing things that are going as we want them to as well as things that aren't. This helps us to remain grounded and retain perspective, building on Chapters 1 and 2. Then when the happy accident occurs we are more likely to notice it.

Tool Two: Morning Pages to Develop Intuition

The second approach is to develop our intuition. The Morning Pages tool of Chapter 2 has already described how to achieve this.

Tool Three: Seeing a Problem as an Opportunity

The third way to become better at finding solutions in adversity is to consciously reinterpret each problem as an opportunity. To achieve this, follow this deceptively simple two-step process.

First, redefine the problem in a way that generalises or expands your viewpoint. You might find that Tool Two of Chapter 2 ('Resolving Our Mis-blinks') is a useful way to achieve this.

Then ask, "Who would find this 'problem' useful?" or "How or where would this 'problem' become an 'advantage'?"

For example, by generalising their descriptions of the apparent problem, the engineers with the leaky tunnel might have switched from asking, "Who would value 'flooding'?" to asking, "Who would value 'water that has been filtered through a mountain'?" Instead of asking, "How can we sell these 'tents'?", Levi Strauss might have asked his team, "What other uses do people around here have for 'hard-wearing cloth'?" And instead of asking, "Who would find 'failed petri dish experiments' useful?", Alexander Fleming might have asked, "Who would find it useful to have 'something that prevents bacteria from growing'?" In the case of Velcro we know that having noticed the burrs attached strongly to his clothes, George de Mestral realised this functionality could be useful, used a microscope to examine the tiny hooks, and then set about finding ways to manufacture them.

With hindsight these examples might seem trivial or obvious. But like the judgments or blinkered thinking of Chapter 2, seeing situations as problems is a mis-blink that is often tricky to spot while you are still in it. Yes, there are negative aspects but there are also always positive ones. Like the mis-blinks tool, this simple approach offers a way to realise that no situation is ever 100 percent a 'problem'. There are always alternative interpretations, if you can spot them.

Side Benefits of Looking for Opportunities

We're not going to discover penicillin or invent blue jeans with every tricky situation we face. But the attitude of approaching problems as if they were opportunities brings us five side benefits, even if we don't find a transformative solution:

1. Inspiration

Seeking to do more than simply remove the problem creates inspiration. "A leader," Napoleon said, "is a dealer in hope." This kind of positive attitude is exciting to be around. It is good for morale and leads to improved productivity and results.

2. Understanding

Searching for the opportunities in a situation forces us to look past surface symptoms and let go of our judgments (which may be mis-blinks). When we dig deeper to identify the fundamentals and ask, "What are we trying to achieve? What specifically is stopping us? How? Where else might that be useful?" we gain a deeper understanding. That understanding will be useful even if we don't find a transformative solution.

3. Durability and Impact

When John Cleese was writing sketches with the Monty Python team, his colleagues would often stop when they got to the first punchline. Cleese would keep working until he found the second, third, or fifth level of comedy. This was harder work and took longer, but the results he created were deeper, more effective, and longer lasting. If you want to generate outcomes that are more remarkable, last longer, or work at a deeper level, learn to think differently and look beyond the first solution or quick fix.

4. Choice and Control

By looking for the opportunities in a situation you retain more control over your own destiny. The opportunities you find bring you new possibilities to choose from. Then, even if the way forward you select is not ideal, you know it is the best choice available and it is *you* who is making the choice.

5. Antifragility

Looking for the opportunities in any situation is a step towards making us and our organisations what Nassim Nicholas Taleb calls 'antifragile'. Fragile, we all know, is a word that describes objects, people, or organisations that break under stress. Objects, people, and organisations that survive under stress we call resilient, strong, or robust. And people and organisations that actually become stronger and more capable when placed under stress, Taleb calls antifragile.

This is what *The Churning* is ultimately all about: creating leaders and organisations that are antifragile, able to use the stress of a situation to become stronger and more capable.

This process begins with the ability to centre, ground, and make sense of the situation. It continues here, when we look for opportunities, build inspiration, deepen our understanding, improve the durability and effectiveness of our responses, and so give ourselves more choices.

We will return to antifragility in Chapter 8.

Five Kinds of Opportunities

We now know that problems contain opportunities and that opportunities bring the inspiration that inner leadership is all about. We know that seeking these opportunities improves morale and puts us back in control, and we've also seen some examples. The next question is, what kinds of opportunity should we look for? It turns out there are five basic types (and then five supplementary ones).

The first two options are to ignore the problem (live with it) or walk away (exit the situation). These might seem unremarkable, or perhaps not proper 'opportunities', but it is worth mentioning them explicitly because we often overlook them. They remind us that we don't have to fix every issue that arises. Sometimes taking no action will send an important message about our priorities to customers, employees, suppliers, or shareholders. Sometimes it is appropriate to do nothing so that other people will take responsibility. Sometimes ignoring a problem is the best thing to do simply because we have other higher priorities to deal with, or because the best we can achieve is to choose which problem we want to live with. Alternatively, if we have been dissatisfied with a situation for a long time, it may make sense to leave that situation and focus our energies elsewhere. This will bring a different set of issues to deal with, but they may teach us more, reward us better, or point us in a direction that we care more about.

If we decide we do want to do something to change an issue, there are three more types of opportunity we can look for.

One is to fix the problem. This means removing the issue and returning the situation to the way it was before the issue arose. In the examples given above this might have meant draining the water from the tunnel, taking the tents to somewhere where tents were needed, washing out the failed petri dishes, and so on. For business leaders this equates to getting the organisation out of the ditch and back on the same track it was on before: fixing the customer relationship, repairing the broken equipment, cutting costs, raising prices, or whatever. These are the standard responses.

Another type of opportunity is to address the issue in a way that improves on the original situation. Most of the innovation examples given above are this kind of response: bottling the mountain-filtered water, turning the tents into jeans, inventing Velcro, and so on. This response is about getting the organisation out of the ditch, and at the same time making it more productive or pointing it in a better direction. Corporate turnarounds and diversifications are often this kind of response.

A final type of response is to resolve or transform the situation in a way that prevents the issue from arising again. The invention of refrigeration is an example of this. Rather than finding better ways to throw away the rotting food, someone eventually asked themselves, "How could we prevent the food from rotting?" This question probably seems obvious to us now but would you have thought of it if you had never seen a refrigerator?

Calling in the maintenance team to fix the broken heating or air-conditioning system is an example of the 'fix' type of response. Organising that team to carry out preventative maintenance is an 'improve' approach. Redesigning the building with increased insulation or natural ventilation so that it doesn't need heating or cooling is an example of the 'transform' approach.

Applying this thinking to product innovation, when Sony invented the Walkman and CD-Walkman these were smaller, more portable ways of playing existing cassettes and CDs, a 'fix' or 'maintain' response. When the MP3 player did away with the need for CDs and tapes, this was an 'improve' response. And Spotify is a 'transform' innovation because it does away with the need to have any specialised player device, as well as the CD or tape.

For organisations, occupancy rates can be a problem in the hotel, airline, and taxi industries. Advertising and promotions can provide a short-term 'fix' that boosts occupancy levels. An 'improve' response would be to increase occupancy by pointing the organisation in a new direction and focusing on a particular group of customers (such as low cost or luxury). And Airbnb and Uber are the 'resolve' or 'transform' type of solution because they do away with the need for the company to own any taxis or hotels, and hence the need to even care about occupancy rates.

Notice that, like good comedy, the improve and transform types of innovation are harder to find. They are also more transformational and disruptive if you can find them.

If you are facing a crisis or problem situation, your five possible responses are:

1. Ignore the Problem or Live With the Situation
When addressing the situation is not a priority for you, or not-addressing it *is* a priority.

2. Leave the Situation
Exit that market. Fire that customer/employer. Go somewhere else to address a set of issues that teach you more, reward you better, or that you care more about.

3. Fix, Restore, or Maintain the Situation
Remove the problem and get things back to how they were before.

4. Improve the Situation
Improve the situation compared to how it was before, by facing or focusing in a new direction.

5. Resolve or Transform the Situation
Do something that prevents the situation arising again.

It might not always be clear which category a solution fits into. That doesn't matter. The point is to use the categories as triggers and catalysts to help you find more ways forward. It is the opportunities and inspiration you find that are important, not which category they fit into.

You won't be able to find the equivalent of refrigeration or Airbnb with every issue you face but, by knowing what to look for, you widen your options and gain the side benefits listed above.

When you look for these alternatives and actively choose among them, you put yourself back in control of your destiny. You give yourself the ability to choose what is best for you in the circumstances that have arisen.

Tool Four: Identify Your Current Opportunities

Let's take what we have just learned and apply it to a challenge or problem that you face.

Start by writing a short factual description of the situation or what has happened.

Then use the second tool of Chapter 2 to check for any mis-blinks and create at least one more generalised, more objective description of the situation. The further you can get from your original interpretation of seeing the situation as a 'problem' the more likely you are to find an answer that brings you the results you want. (Some examples are given in the table on page 54.)

Now define the outcome you want to create. Write at least one more objective description of that as well. Again, the more ways you find to generalise this the more chance you give yourself of finding attractive solutions. (The creativity tools of Chapter 1 might be useful.)

Now, remembering the three tools described earlier for developing serendipity, intuition, and seeing the problem as an opportunity, list as many options as you can for responding to the situation.

At this stage it doesn't matter how feasible or attractive the ideas seem. The point is to play with them, find alternatives, and see what inspires you. Even the ideas that seem unattractive bring useful information about the kinds of outcomes you don't want. And a crazy idea may lead to a better one.

When you can think of no more ideas, group them under the five types of opportunity: Ignore, Leave, Fix, Improve, Transform. Don't worry if it's not quite clear which category an idea comes under: it's the ideas that matter, not the categories they belong to. Choose whichever seems best. Does this trigger more ideas?

Are most of the ideas grouped under the same one or two categories? Are there any categories with no ideas?

Finally, *taking the categories in reverse order*, find at least one more idea for each group. What would it take to Transform or Resolve the situation so it couldn't arise again? What would be a way to Improve the situation over how it was before? And so on.

Use the tools for serendipity, intuition, and seeing the problem as an opportunity. Remember John Cleese: the best answers come from persistence to look beyond the obvious. Stretch to five new ideas per category if you can, no matter how outlandish they might seem at first.

The table below contains some hypothetical examples, based on three of the situations mentioned earlier: the tunnellers, jeans, and penicillin. Notice how the initial descriptions of the situation can easily contain the mis-blinks discussed in Chapter 2 ("disaster… stupidly… failed"). Generalising the issue helps to remove these mis-blinks.

Notice that in the case of penicillin, what we might imagine as the 'ideal' transformative outcome ("preventing the situation from ever arising again") would have led to improved sterilisation procedures for the petri dishes, and the loss of millions of lives. There is no 'best' or 'right' answer to aim for here. There is only identifying as many alternatives as possible, so that you maximise your ability to choose what is best for you in the circumstances.

As another example, imagine what an executive at Sony's head office might have thought in 2011 when floods hit their suppliers in Thailand. Their initial reaction might have been "Complete disaster! Our factories have flooded!" Generalising this description would have created the less personal, less emotive, "Factories across the whole region have flooded." The outcome the executive wanted instead might then have been to keep their people safe and get their supply chain operating again.

Type 1 opportunities to Live With the situation might have included, "Not my responsibility, leave it to the people on the ground" or "Do nothing until the waters have receded."

Type 2 opportunities to Exit the situation might have included finding new suppliers, either temporarily or permanently.

	Tunnellers	Levis Strauss	Alexander Fleming
Possible Description of the Problem	- Complete disaster! Leaks are preventing trains from running	- I stupidly forgot it doesn't rain here, people don't need my products	- Some of the dish culture experiments failed
More Generic Ways to Describe the 'Problem'	- We have a plentiful source of mountain-filtered water	- I have a stock of hard-wearing fabric and customers who need other things from what I thought they did	- Bacteria did not grow on some dishes - Something unusual and interesting stopped the bacteria growing
Ways to Describe What You Want Instead	- Enable trains to run through the tunnel - Remove the water	- Find a new market for the tents - Find a local use for hard-wearing fabric	- Have bacteria grow perfectly every time - Understand root causes of why bacteria didn't grow
Ways to Do Nothing or Live With the Situation	- Slow trains as they enter the tunnel - Use different trains	- Reduce prices - Give tents away - Barter the tents	- Leave failed dishes out of results
Ways to Leave the Situation	- Close the tunnel and build another in a drier place	- Give up on being an entrepreneur - Get a job	- Change the experiment - Get another job
Ways to Fix or Maintain the Situation	- Install pumps or drains - Create waterproof inner tunnel	- Take the tents to somewhere rainy	- Wash the dishes and repeat the experiment
Ways to Improve the Situation **(Who would find it useful?)**	- Bottle the water - Sell water to farmers - Generate electricity?	- Cut sides off tents, sell as sun shades - Sell fabric as jeans	- Investigate why the bacteria didn't grow - Give/sell penicillin to the world
Ways to Transform or Resolve the Situation	- Invent machine that seals tunnel as it drills	- ??	- Improve sterilising procedures

Type 3 opportunities to Fix the situation back to how it was before the floods would have included all the different options for getting existing suppliers up and running again.

Type 4 opportunities to Improve the situation over how it was before might have included using the disaster as an opportunity to bring forward plans to modernise the factories, perhaps funded by insurance.

Type 5 opportunities to Transform the situation so that it could not happen again might have included building a wall around the site(s), installing pumps, working with others to improve flood defences in the region, shifting the factories to new locations, or pushing for global action on climate change.

Finally, as an individual example, let's imagine an executive who unexpectedly finds herself without a job at the age of 55.

Her initial reaction might be "They have fired me as Vice President of Widget Sales!" A more neutral, generic way of saying the same thing could be, "That role has come to an end sooner than I expected and I notice I am experiencing churning so I will centre and ground." The person might also broaden her description of herself from "I am VP of Widget Sales" to "I am person with proven skills in managing teams, understanding client needs, identifying solutions that fulfil those needs, building relationships, convincing clients to buy, as well as some knowledge of widgets."

What she now wants to find might be a role that brings a certain combination of salary, personal fulfilment, creating a legacy, working close to home, and so on.

Type 1 opportunities here might include taking a couple of months' holiday or vacation, or taking an interim or part-time job. Both are ways to Do Nothing about finding a new full-time position.

Type 2 opportunities could include selling up and moving abroad, joining a commune, or retiring early. All are ways to Exit the situation of 'having a job'.

Type 3 opportunities, to Fix or Restore the situation back to how it was before, would include looking for similar roles in similar companies.

Type 4 opportunities, to Improve the situation over how it was before, would include seeking out more responsible roles in the same industry, or transferring into a different, more attractive industry.

Type 5 opportunities to Transform the situation so that it could not happen again might include starting her own firm or becoming a speaker or consultant, all ways in which 'being fired' could not happen again.

What she eventually did was become president of her city's blockchain association (Type 4) and a speaker and consultant (Type 5). But there are many other possibilities and different people will find different options more and less attractive at different times.

So centre and ground, make clear sense of your situation, and accept it as it is. Then use the five categories to look for what inspires *you* about the way the world could be.

The more you look, the more ways you will find to move forward. And like John Cleese, the more ideas you come up with, the more likely you are to find inspiration.

You probably now have at least five alternative ways forward. Each will bring a mix of upsides and downsides, benefits and disadvantages, and you might decide to pursue more than one of them.

Now let's look at five more.

Five More Opportunities for You

Ten years ago the challenges you face today would probably not have arisen for you. You were likely in a different role and didn't have the skills or experience to be able do what you can do today. In the same way, things that you found challenging then are probably easy and routine for you now.

Your abilities to lead yourself and others today have grown directly out of the challenges you faced in the past. This means the challenges you face now are also opportunities to develop into the kind of person you want to become. Each situation brings with it not only the opportunity to create new results but also the opportunity to develop your skills and abilities.

This brings you five more options for moving forward, which are:

6.　Ignore: Don't Apply the leadership skills you have
You can choose to ignore or live with a situation (by not applying your existing leadership skills) when resolving that situation is not a priority for you, or when deliberately not resolving it will create the outcome you want.

7. Remove your leadership skills to somewhere else
This means taking your leadership skills and applying them in a different role, perhaps one that has more meaning for you, or that better matches your needs, or will develop or reward you better.

8. Maintain: Apply your existing leadership skills
This means applying the leadership abilities you already have (to then fix, improve, or transform the situation).

9. Improve your ability to lead yourself and others
Use the situation as an opportunity to develop your skills, competencies, and abilities.

10. Transform your leadership
Acquire the skills that would have prevented the situation from happening in the first place. If you can't think of what those skills are, imagine a leader you admire, ask yourself what they would have done to avoid the situation arising, then learn to copy that.

Here are some examples of how these five responses might have applied to the Sony executive and the Vice President of Sales.

For the Sony executive, Not-Applying his leadership would have meant focusing on something else while allowing others to deal with the flooding. For the VP of Sales, this option might have meant recharging her batteries with a holiday or vacation, or taking a more junior role on a temporary basis. These answers are similar to the opportunities we already identified using the first five categories, but that doesn't matter. In other cases, looking at the situation from the leadership perspective may identify new ideas.

Removing your leadership means taking your leadership elsewhere. For the Sony executive this could have meant resigning. For the VP of Sales, early retirement would have been a way to remove her leadership skills from the job market.

The third option, Applying Existing leadership skills, would have meant the Sony executive becoming involved in the flooding in a way that was appropriate to his position, and the VP of Sales looking for a role as VP of Sales in a similar firm.

Using the situation as an opportunity to Improve his ability to lead himself and others could have meant the Sony executive jumping in to handle a larger crisis than he had done before. Or it might have meant him stepping back and improving his ability to coach others to handle the situation. For the VP of Sales, this Improve option might have meant shifting into a different industry, becoming a CEO, leading a startup, or retraining in many other directions. It could also have meant applying the tools of *Inner Leadership* to improve her ability to handle her emotional reactions to not having a job, make clear sense of the situation, and create an inspiring vision of what she most wanted to do next.

Finally, the fifth opportunity for developing our leadership is probably the most important. If we can Transform our leadership to prevent a situation from arising in the first place then we have achieved true skill. As Sun Tzu wrote in *The Art of War* more than 2,000 years ago, "The greatest victory is that which requires no battle. Supreme excellence is to subdue the enemy without fighting."

For the Sony executive, this option would have meant preventing flooding from happening again, by raising his game to address a larger locus of control than he had considered for his role before: perhaps tackling the issue of flooding across the region, or taking action to address climate change. For the VP of sales this could have meant developing her political skills, to reduce her likelihood of being fired in future, or simply joining an organisation she cared more passionately about, and which would need her passion in return.

In Chapter 4 I describe a personal example of a challenge that became an opportunity for me to develop my inner leadership in this way. (It fits better with the material of that chapter but if you want to read it now it's on page 72.)

Tool Five: Opportunities to Lead Yourself and Others

Each of the five options for applying your leadership is a different way of thinking about the situation. By thinking through all five you push your thinking past the obvious solutions and 'outside the box'.

Each option you identify is a step towards finding a new possibility. And each alternative you find brings more clarity on what you do and do not want from the way forward you eventually choose.

Look again at the situation you described in Tool Four. Identify as many opportunities as you can for applying or developing your leadership abilities in each of the five directions.

Start by thinking big. How might you:

10. Transform your ability to lead, so that you can prevent a similar situation from happening again.
9. Improve or Develop your ability to lead yourself and others
8. Apply the leadership abilities you already have
7. Remove your leadership, take it elsewhere
6. Not Apply your leadership

The opportunities you find this time are not about changing outcomes but about changing the attitudes and intention with which you respond to a situation. They are about the emotional energy you bring, the attitude that defines your inner leadership. And no matter what the situation, you always have a choice about that.

Not every idea will be appropriate. The point is to realise that you have a choice, emotionally as well as practically, about whether you respond to a situation as a 'crisis' or an 'opportunity'. The choice you make will then affect the emotions and morale of the people around you, as well as the outcomes you are likely to get.

It can be useful to think about past situations. Have you tended to follow a pattern in the way you responded to past challenges? Have you often jumped in to fix them, even when someone else might have learned from the experience or when someone else was responsible? Have you tended to walk away from difficult issues? Or ignored them in the hope that they would go away? Do you have a habit of burning yourself out by stretching for transformative solutions that no one else is interested in? Do the ideas you are coming up with today repeat the same pattern? Is that appropriate? Might it be useful to look harder for other options before you decide what route to take?

As before, by identifying alternatives you increase your chances of finding the way forward that inspires you most.

No matter what options you identify, notice how your ability to handle outer challenges for the organisation is bound up with your inner capability as a leader. The one expands the other. Choosing to pursue new results will require you to develop your abilities as a leader. Developing new abilities as a leader will enable you to deliver new results. Every challenge you face is also an opportunity.

You probably now have at least ten possible directions for moving forward. Each brings a mix of upsides and downsides, benefits and disadvantages.

In Chapter 4 we will look at how to choose among them.

Big Problems Bring Big Opportunities

Steve Jobs was an imperfect human being like the rest of us, but he achieved more in his short lifetime than many of us do.

In his famous commencement address at Stanford in 2005, Jobs talked about how his biggest challenge contained an even larger opportunity.

When Jobs was 30, the company he had founded and worked hard in all his adult life fired him. It was, he said, "devastating."

For a few months Jobs felt awful, "a very public failure." But then he reflected and decided to start over. "It turned out," he said, "that getting fired from Apple was the best thing that could have ever happened to me. The heaviness of being successful was replaced by the lightness of being a beginner again... It freed me to enter one of the most creative periods of my life... It was awful tasting medicine, but I guess the patient needed it."

He also gave advice for anyone finding themselves in a similar situation. "Sometimes life hits you in the head with a brick," he said. "Don't lose faith. I'm convinced that the only thing that kept me going was that I loved what I did. You've got to find what you love... If you haven't found it yet, keep looking. Don't settle."

For Steve Jobs, his biggest problem contained his biggest opportunity, even though he couldn't see that at first. And for him, the way forward became clear only after he found what most inspired him, what he most loved.

Conclusions

This chapter has been about identifying the opportunities that exist in any situation. If you have experienced any churning while reading it, remember to use the tools of Chapter 1 to centre and ground.

Whether we see a situation as a problem or an opportunity shapes the way that we respond. But the story of the Taoist farmer shows that this is always an interpretation: we can never tell how a situation is going to turn out. It is we who decide whether to interpret a certain turn of events as an opportunity or a crisis.

Often we make that choice unconsciously, a mis-blink from Chapter 2. But any situation always contains a mix of opportunities as well as threats. By learning to develop our serendipity, intuition, and the ability to see problems as solutions, we make ourselves more likely to find the opportunities. We give ourselves an opportunity mindset. We live like Doctor Who and turn each crisis into an adventure.

No matter what opportunities we find, the benefits of simply looking for upsides include improved morale, better understanding, increased durability, greater control, and antifragility. Looking for opportunities is simply good leadership: "A leader is a dealer in hope."

There are always five potential ways in which we might respond to a situation:

1. Ignore or Live With the situation
2. Leave or Exit the situation
3. Fix, Maintain, or Restore the situation
4. Improve the situation
5. Transform or Resolve the situation

And there are always five potential opportunities for applying or developing our leadership skills:

6. Not Apply our leadership
7. Remove our leadership, take it elsewhere
8. Apply the leadership abilities we already have
9. Improve or Develop our ability to lead ourselves and others
10. Transform our ability to lead, by acquiring the skills needed to prevent a similar situation from happening again

The more alternatives we identify, the more options we give ourselves for choosing how to respond, the more deeply we understand what our priorities are, and the more likely it is that we will find a way forward that inspires us.

Steve Jobs showed how even the biggest crisis can contain a massive opportunity. The key, he said, is to find what you love, find what inspires you.

In Chapter 4 we will review the opportunities you have identified and choose the one that is best for you.

Measurement

Have you identified more opportunities to move forward from your current situation than you were aware of before you read this chapter? Have you increased the number of positive potential outcomes? Do you feel more confident that you have examined all the possibilities?

On a scale of 0 to 10, how able are you now to spot the opportunities in a crisis? How does this compare with where you were at the start of the chapter?

What differences will this make in your life? What benefits will that bring? How valuable is that to you?

Is it a priority for you to strengthen these abilities further? Why? How much time will you allocate to achieving this?

Measuring Inner Leadership

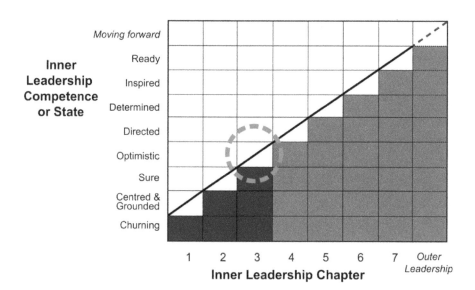

4. Choose What's Best For You

This chapter marks the half way point on our journey. It describes the pivot point, the go/no-go decision, the tipping point of inner leadership.

We began the book by saying that we are living through a time of unprecedented change. We imagined ourselves facing some kind of challenge or crisis and then we centred, grounded, and deepened our connection with ourselves. We made clear sense of the situation, resolving mis-blinks and spotting new patterns. And then we looked for the ten types of opportunity that exist in any situation.

This chapter is about deciding which of those opportunities you want to pursue: your future direction of travel. In the chapters that follow, you will then compare that choice against your purpose and values, turn it into an inspiring vision, and prepare for implementation.

If you already know which opportunity from Chapter 3 you want to pursue you might want to skip ahead to the tools (page 75), which are important preparation for the later chapters.

Alternatively, if you haven't yet chosen your best way forward, or if you want to learn how you and other people can make faster, clearer decisions in times of change, read on.

This chapter is about deciding where you want to get to and why. It is about identifying the way forward that is best for you personally and making the commitment to follow that path.

The chapter has three sections: why this choice matters, why we sometimes get stuck, and how to get unstuck.

Before we begin, on a scale of 0 to 10, how do you rate your current ability to choose and pursue the best way forward for you?

Why this Choice Matters

A Deep Pattern of Our Culture: To Be or Not to Be

At the core of this chapter is an idea, a pattern, a meme that runs through almost every aspect of our culture and our life-experience. It drives our advertising and determines the products and services we buy. It shapes the work we do, the jobs and careers we select, and the people who we choose to be our friends, lovers, and life-partners.

Our culture is so infused with this idea that you might almost say it *is* our culture. And yet, because it is so tied up with the very essence of our human experience, like fish surrounded by water, we hardly notice it is there.

This is the pattern that gave Shakespeare his most famous line, "To be, or not to be." This is the idea that summarises the defining mantra of the most powerful nation on Earth, the American Dream that you can become anything you want to. This is the meme that describes the universal structure of the Hero's Journey that runs through *Star Wars*, *Casablanca*, *Breaking Bad*, and almost every spellbinding, bestselling story ever told.

The most talked-about, invisible, pattern of our culture is the idea that we might one day grow to fulfil our destiny, our identity.

Who we think we are determines the clothes we wear, the car we drive (or don't), the food we eat, the homes and neighbourhoods we live in, and the schools we send our children to.

It determines the directions we choose to move forward in: whether we take the well-worn path or the road less travelled.

And the difference between who we are being now and our often unconscious sense of who we might want to become is what brings the tension that we notice from time to time: the sometimes indefinable, sometimes intense feeling that we need to make a change in our life.

Like all living things we are striving to become, even if we are not always fully aware of what that means.

Engaging at this deep level is not something we do often. But a time of change brings a series of challenges that are also opportunities: to look deeper and find out more about ourselves. The tools in this book show us how to do this and convert that understanding into action. They provide a framework not only for leading better in a time of change but also for becoming the person we most want to be: a framework for individuation and self-actualisation.

This chapter is about getting clearer on who you most want to become and choosing your most appropriate next step towards that.

A Note on Destiny

The word destiny means different things to different people so I want to be clear about the meaning I am using here.

The English word destiny comes from the French word *destinée* and shares the same original root as *destination*. It looks to the future, to the place that we are trying to reach.

For some people, destiny is something already pre-ordained, fated, or fixed and the original Latin word *destinare* did indeed mean "to make firm or establish." But over time the meaning shifted to become "the action of intending someone or something for a purpose."

We all have different inner dictionaries defining what we think words mean. In this book, the way I am using the word destiny isn't about something being fixed or pre-ordained. It's about making a choice or setting an intention, for a purpose we will return to in the next chapter.

Human Becomings

Think back through your life. At the age of 16 you were not the same person as you had been when you were six. Nor were you the same at 16 as you were (or will be) at 26, 36, or 66, though something about us stays the same.

We are not simply human beings, we are human becomings. Throughout our lives, in different ways and at different rates, we are always changing and becoming.

The person who we try to become, the lives we try to lead, and the degree to which we are aided or held back from doing so, are all influenced by the culture of the people around us and the times we happen to have been born into. If you had been born into a different century, a different country, or even a different family, you would see the world differently from the way you do now.

Sometimes we are happy with who we are. Sometimes there is a gap between who we are being and the person we want to become. It is this *inner* gap that catches us when we hear the words, "To be or not to be," when someone whispers in our ear, "You can be anything you want to," or when we get caught up in the Hero's Journey, told and retold in countless movies, novels, and television programmes.

The reason why "To be or not to be," the American Dream, and the Hero's Journey continue to play such a compelling part of our culture is because they are echoes and reflections of our own inner will or drive to become. They resonate with our equivalent of a seed's yearning to grow into a plant, a caterpillar's drive to transform into a butterfly, the urge to become that is part of what it means to be alive.

We all know what a seed and caterpillar want to become, but what about a human being? If who we think we are is shaped by the century, country, and family we happen to be born into, how can we look past these symptoms to find out who we really are?

Sigmund Freud taught us that life is love and work. Success for a human being is about being able to love and be loved, and to find work that we do well. To this, psychologist Will Schutz added a third dimension he called significance: we all want to do or be someone or something that matters.

These three factors together are what drive all human beings forward: love, work, and significance. We all want to love and be loved. We all want to do work that uses and develops our unique talents. And we all want to matter to someone or something, somewhere, on whatever scale is right for us.

Expressed in different ways, these three factors lie at the heart of what we all seek. We don't always find ourselves in the perfect conditions to achieve these things. But like a plant growing through concrete, we strive on anyway. This is how we become.

Let's use this understanding to find out what happens when a person living through a time of churning finds themselves in a difficult situation.

Understanding What Makes an Opportunity or a Crisis

Let's imagine, as a worst case scenario, a leader who is facing some sort of extreme crisis that is making her or him experience inner churning.

First let's centre and ground. Then let's use Chapter 2 to take away the judgment word 'crisis' and replace it with the longer but more accurately descriptive words "situation that is taking the leader outside their ability to handle it as routine, and is affecting them emotionally."

As before, the reason the situation is upsetting the person's emotional balance is because it is resonating with their inner world: either with who they think they are or who they want to become. More specifically, remembering Freud and Schutz, the event will create an emotional response when the leader *thinks* it means something about their competence, their significance, or their likeability.

People who interpret a situation as meaning that they or their team will be seen as less capable, less important, or less popular will call it a problem or crisis. Situations where businesses go bankrupt, make less profit, or lose market share are often seen as crises.

Conversely, situations that show a leader or their team as more competent, more important, or more popular we call opportunities. Scenarios where we can increase profits, grow market share, or show our service is better than competitors' are often seen as opportunities.

And a situation that doesn't imply anything either way is a non-event, business as usual, neither a crisis nor an opportunity.

This shows the root cause of why we see some situations as crises or threats and others as opportunities. As we said in Chapters 2 and 3 it has nothing to do with the situation. It's all about the *interpretation* we make about what the situation means for our identity.

But the story of the Taoist farmer shows that we can never know whether a situation will turn out to be a crisis or an opportunity. And Chapter 3 shows that opportunities are formed from the choices we make about how to combine external events with our inner capabilities.

The net result of all these choices determines where we end up: our destiny. So if the leader we imagined facing the 'extreme crisis' wants to control what that destiny looks like, he needs to centre and ground, let go of the churning he is creating for himself, understand the situation more clearly, identify the ten types of opportunity that exist alongside the threat, and then choose the option that is the best choice for now to take him towards his preferred destiny.

Peter Drucker had a very clear opinion about how to do this. He was an author and consultant whose thinking made a major contribution to the foundation of the modern business corporation. He said, "Doing the right things is more important than doing things right."

For our leader who is facing the extreme crisis this means two things. First, it is important for him to be clear about what the 'right things' are for him: the destiny he wants to create. Second, it is better to choose an imperfect path towards that destiny than to choose an easy path that will take him in a different direction.

The tools in the third section of this chapter will enable you to gain clarity both on the destiny you want and which of the options you identified in Chapter 3 is the best way forward for you now.

But before we come to those tools, we first need to make sure that we will be able to commit fully to the choice we make.

Testing the Model and Its Implications:

Let's pause for a moment and test what you just read. Is it really true that "an event will create an emotional response in a leader when they think it means something about their competence, significance, or likeability"?

Think of at least one opportunity and one crisis you faced. Did you imagine that you or your team would be associated with some of the following words or their opposites?

Competent: Capable, talented, celebrity, skilful, winning, intelligent, smart, experienced, respected, results-oriented, trusted, and opposites such as incompetent, useless, failure, …

Significant: Successful, special, leading, large, chief, senior, head, important, influential, powerful, prominent, respected, rich, famous, celebrity, trending, notorious, and opposites such as irrelevant, weak, powerless, poor, …

Likeable: Popular, well-liked, much-loved, fashionable, charismatic, famous, attractive, celebrated, celebrity, loveable, trending, and opposites such as hated, despised, notorious, …

Notice that some words ('celebrity') contain a mix of meanings.

Notice also that words like notorious mean "significant, but in a bad way." For some people it doesn't matter whether they are famous or infamous, just so long as they have the attention. Others are driven by a need to be liked or seen as talented.

By becoming aware of these three inner drivers we can learn to grow past them. We are all loveable, we are all capable at something, and we can all find a role where we can make a difference, be significant.

The more grounded a person becomes in trusting their own competence, significance, and likeability the less they will care what others think. The less they will then see any situation as a 'crisis' or an 'opportunity'. In the words of Rudyard Kipling's poem *If*, they will "meet with Triumph and Disaster, And treat those two impostors just the same." They will focus simply on finding the opportunities in the situation and choosing what fits best with their chosen destiny.

That is what *Inner Leadership*, and this chapter in particular, is teaching us to do.

Three Reasons Why
We Sometimes Get Stuck

We are all human becomings and the person we become is the result of all the choices we make. If we choose to centre, ground, and make sense of the situation then we now know how to find the opportunities, even in a crisis. But, in spite of this, some people can still sometimes get stuck.

This section is about understanding why that happens. It is about giving us the tools to let go of those blockages (if we need to) so that we can choose the most appropriate way forward for us now and turn it into an inspiring vision.

The three main reasons why people can sometimes get stuck are:

• Overthinking
• Not knowing who we want to become
• Fear

Overthinking

Overthinking is paralysis by analysis: endlessly flipping back and forth between alternatives and their possible consequences, wondering what to do, but never actually doing anything.

The classic example of this comes from Shakespeare's play *Hamlet*. It is clear early on that Hamlet's uncle has killed his father and married his mother but instead of taking revenge Hamlet overthinks what to do. "Is it nobler," he wonders, "to suffer the slings and arrows of outrageous fortune, or to take arms against a sea of troubles, and by opposing end them?" If he took action would he succeed, or would death become an endless time "to sleep, perchance to dream"?

As he dithers over whether "to be or not to be," events move on around him until suddenly, oops!: "I am dead, Horatio."

A wasted opportunity.

We all recognise this, which is why we love the play. And the living death that Hamlet achieves by not taking action is in a way worse than the actual death he eventually suffers anyway. He accomplishes nothing by dithering and the play is a tragedy in the truest sense.

"To be or not to be" truly is the question. Or rather, "to become or not to become." We will never be perfect, and we will never know 100 percent how things are going to turn out, especially in a time of churning. The point, as Drucker said, is to "do the right things": to know what is most important to us and to see how far we can get at achieving that. To take our best shot at *becoming* what matters most to us, creating the future we most want, given the imperfect place we are all starting from today.

The mis-blinks tool of Chapter 2 would have helped Hamlet shift to action, by highlighting his 'shoulds', assumptions, and the extreme thinking of being able to see only total success or utter failure. He could also have used the Morning Pages to think through his options.

If, instead of asking "To be or not to be?", Hamlet had used Chapter 2 to make sense of his situation, Chapter 3 to identify his alternatives, and then chosen the best way forward for him (even if it wasn't perfect), we would have lost a famous soliloquy but gained a more life-filled ending.

Not Knowing Who We Want to Become

A second way that people can sometimes get stuck is when they aren't sure who or what they want to become. This lack of clarity about direction and purpose can make all options seem equally (ir)relevant, which can then also lead to indecision and overthinking.

The more you have used the grounding and deepening tools of Chapter 1 to build a deeper connection with who you are, what you care about, and who you want to become, the clearer the differences between your options for moving forward will be. The Morning Pages of Chapter 2 also provide a way to think through alternatives. Both will make your choice easier, even if implementation seems difficult. (And in a time of churning, all ways forward may seem difficult.)

This adds another option to your list of opportunities: to 'Live with' the situation for a while as you get clearer on who you want to become. If you choose this option, be sure it doesn't turn into a way of avoiding a decision. Set limits. Be clear on what clarity you will obtain, by when, and how you will go about doing so. Then take the best decision you can. If there is no particular date by when you need to take a decision, ask yourself whether it really is a priority and why.

Remember that it is better to have done the work on this *before* you need the answer. Chapters 1 and 2 began the process. The tools in the next section provide more insights. And Chapter 5 will bring additional clarity. But ultimately it is only by moving forward, down any path, that we learn the reality of what we like and don't like, and so gain greater clarity about who we want to become.

Fear

Most of all, the third reason we can find ourselves stuck is simply that we are afraid. Afraid to fail and afraid to succeed.

As Marianne Williamson famously told us in her book *Return to Love* (which is also often quoted as coming from Nelson Mandela's Inauguration Speech in 1994):

> "Our deepest fear is not that we are inadequate. Our deepest fear is that we are powerful beyond measure. It is our light, not our darkness that most frightens us. We ask ourselves, who am I to be brilliant, gorgeous, talented, fabulous? Actually, who are you not to be?"

Our playing small because of fear does not serve us. It does not serve the people around us. And it does not serve the world.

The reality is that the challenges we now face provide an increasing range of opportunities for all of us to step into. And if you don't, who will?

The point of this chapter is to help you identify the challenge or opportunity, no matter how large or small, that is the best way forward for *you* now. Chapter 5 will help you to develop it further, and the rest of *Inner Leadership* will prepare you to implement it. *Outer Leadership* will provide you with the tools to do so.

Chapter 3 already provided two ways to overcome fear. Simply looking for opportunities improves our morale. Listing our options under the ten types of opportunity makes our decision clearer, more objective, more neutral. And then, even if the way forward we choose is not ideal, we know it is the best one available under the current circumstances.

In a churning world all ways forward will be unpredictable. The point is to choose a direction and move towards it, knowing that we will have to pivot later.

By using these tools we can shift our response to fear from "Forget Everything And Run" to "Face Everything And Rise."

A Personal Example of 'The Challenge Is The Opportunity'

At this point you might be thinking it is all very well saying "the challenge is the opportunity" but it's not so easy putting that into practice.

Not long ago I would have agreed with you, so it is probably useful to give an example here of how I applied this principle in my own life. It's an example of how one major challenge I faced became an opportunity, but only after I had overcome all three of the blockages outlined above.

Just as I was about to start writing this book I was diagnosed as possibly having the same cancer that had recently killed my father. A couple of other things were going on in my life at the same time, so it was not good news, not good timing, and I found it extremely emotionally upsetting.

I also knew that the test isn't 100 percent reliable. A positive result doesn't necessarily mean you have the disease. And even if you do, the best thing might be simply to leave it alone because treatment can cause significant, lasting, negative impacts on quality of life.

It was a bit like being told that even though my car was running perfectly now there *might* be a problem with it in ten years' time. Or there might not. And if I took the car in for service then the mechanics *might* be able to fix it, or they might not. But they also had a significant track record of messing up other parts of the car at the same time.

The situation was definitely taking me out of my comfort zone.

For a few months, as tests and discussions progressed, I found myself in an increasingly intense double-bind, apparently trapped between "If I do nothing I might die" and "If I do something I might live unpleasantly (and unnecessarily)."

As I churned back and forth between "To operate or not to operate, that is the question," the thought suddenly popped into my head, "The challenge is the opportunity."

"Yeah, right!" I thought. "Thanks for that."

But then I reflected.

I had seen and heard this principle a hundred times before, but I had never really applied it. I had wanted it to be true, but I couldn't see how it was. "The problem is the solution." How does that work?

If it were true, then in facing my biggest challenge I would also be facing my biggest opportunity.

This was definitely a good time to test out the proposition. Either it was true, and I would solve my problem and learn something important. Or it was garbage and I could stop wasting my time.

As I reflected on what the opportunity might be, the first thing I noticed was that my level of inner churning fell dramatically. Somehow, as it says in Chapter 3, simply by looking for an opportunity I immediately felt better, even though nothing in the outer situation had changed. It put me back in control and that helped me face the situation more calmly.

In the end, the biggest opportunity I identified was not to leave the situation or ignore it, nor simply to fix the cancer (the option being recommended by the doctors). Nor was it to make the lifestyle changes that might have prevented the cancer from developing in the first place.

The greatest opportunity for me, I decided, was to change my own thinking: the inner leadership attitude that was keeping me stuck. I realised that my real problem wasn't that I didn't like the alternatives being presented by the doctors. My real problem was that I was keeping myself trapped between those alternatives instead of generating another way forward that I liked better. It wasn't the situation that was upsetting me, it was the feeling of being stuck. And that was something I was creating for myself.

My best opportunity was to stop relying on the opinions of others, merely because they were 'experts', and to take back responsibility for my own healthcare. I might not like the alternatives being presented to me, but it was up to me to find or create another way forward that I wanted more.

In the words of Chapter 3, this was an opportunity to Improve or Transform my inner leader.

In practice, what this meant was that I went on to find consultants who gave me a fourth and then a fifth opinion: ways forward that brought the upsides I wanted without the downsides I didn't.

This experience taught me that the challenge truly is the opportunity. It was a watershed that has since enabled me to sidestep my emotional reactions to several situations, changing my thinking from "This is a difficult situation, how can I get out of it?" to "This is a difficult situation. What is making it difficult? What do I want instead? How can I get that? How much effort am I willing to put in to achieve what outcome(s)?"

With hindsight, I realise that "to operate or not to operate" is actually blinkered extreme thinking from Chapter 2. And with further hindsight, the clarity and tools of all three Chapters 1-3 would have been useful to me. But of course I hadn't written them yet.

Four More Tools for Getting Unstuck

The previous sections discussed why the choice you are about to make matters and why people sometimes get stuck making it. They also described how tools in the earlier chapters have already started to remove the three blockages of overthinking, fear, and not knowing who we want to become.

The four tools in this section will extend this and bring you deeper clarity on who you want to become, and how you can best get there from among the options you identified in Chapter 3.

They achieve this by:
- learning from others
- learning from your past
- learning from your future, and
- comparing your alternative ways forward

The first tool is also important preparation for Chapter 5.

Tool One: Learning from Others

Learning from other people is a good way to identify what's important to us and to remember that even our heroes aren't perfect. This tool will help you gain clarity on who you want to become.

The tool has two parts: learning from people we have met and learning from people we haven't. It is adapted from materials developed by Olivier Mythodrama (www.oliviermythodrama.com).

First, choose one to three people you have never met but who you greatly admire. They might be people from history or from the present day: role models who taught you something important but who you never interacted with.

For each one, write down or (better) discuss with a close friend or partner:
1. What are the values you admire in these people?
2. What flaws or weaknesses did they have?
3. What, despite those flaws, did they manage to achieve that you admire them for?

Discussing this with someone you trust will enable them to draw out what is really important to you by asking open questions such as, "Why? What do you mean by that? Can you give me an example?"

For the second part of the tool, choose one to three mentors, friends, leaders, teachers, or managers you knew in real life who taught you something that has helped to shape the person you have become.

Again, either write down or discuss with a close friend or partner:

1.   What did these people love that you loved them for loving?
2.   What were their flaws or weaknesses?
3.   What, despite those flaws, did they manage to achieve that you admire them for?

Write your answers down or record them in the electronic workbook. You will need them again in Chapter 5.

Reminding yourself of the qualities and achievements you admire in others will help you to choose your own way forward. This tool also reminds us that, like the people we most admire, we don't have to be perfect in order to achieve something worthwhile.

Tool Two: Learning from Your Past

Re-examining events in the past that didn't turn out as we expected can help us to identify what else we might have done. This can bring us new confidence to move forward in whatever situation we currently face, helping to overcome fear and overthinking.

Pick a time in your life when things didn't turn out as you expected. (Remember that even professional forecasters often get it wrong and Thomas Edison tried thousands of ways to make a light bulb before he found one that worked. He saw each so-called 'failure' as another successful step towards finding the outcome he wanted.)

Ask yourself:

• What choice did you make? What did you expect was going to happen? What actually happened?
• What lesson did you learn at the time? Using Chapter 2, was that lesson a mis-blink?
• What alternative explanations are also possible? Which seems more likely?

- What other opportunities might you have chosen: to ignore, leave, fix, improve, or transform the situation or your leadership?
- Would you take the same decision again?

If you would take the same decision then you know that you can trust the choice you make today, even though things might not turn out the way you expect.

If you would take a different decision, then again you can trust the choice you make today, because you have learned from experience in the past and will be able to do so again if needed.

Either way, the best way forward is to choose what is best for you now and act on it.

Tool Three: Learning from Your Future

Life doesn't always turn out the way we expect and as we grow older we generally become wiser. What advice, for example, would you give now to your 6-, 16-, or 26-year-old self? Think about that for a moment.

Then ask yourself what advice your 86-year-old self would give to you now about choosing your best way forward.

One of Peter Drucker's most enduring principles for success is to "Define what finishing well means to you." This is more than Stephen Covey's "Begin with the end in mind." It is about defining not only what 'finished' looks like but also how you are going to reach that end: what it will take for you to finish *well*. Spending time to answer that question now will help you make the choices that lead you there.

To define what finishing well means for you, imagine yourself on your deathbed. What will it take for you to have lived a worthwhile life? To have made good use of your time? To have 'finished well'? Define six to eight aspects or areas of life that are important to you.

When you know your answers you can use them in three ways.

First, when facing a challenging situation, you can ask yourself, "What would my 86-year-old self advise me to do?"

Second, you can ask yourself which way forward now will best take you towards what finishing well looks like for you. (If none do then revisit Chapter 3 with this information in mind and look for new options among the ten types of opportunity.)

Third, you can create a plan to take you from wherever you are now towards whatever finishing well looks like for you:

- For each of the six to eight areas you identified as important, define what 10 looks like on a scale of 0 to 10
- Rate where you are on that scale today (0 to 10)
- Define appropriate activities over the next week, month, or year, that move you towards where you want to finish, or
- Define what would it take to improve by 1 or 0.1 from wherever you are now

Remember that we are all human becomings as well as human beings and in a time of churning the world will not always turn out the way we expect. This means it can make sense to focus less on whether we have got to '10' yet and more on whether we are moving in the direction we want to, given the way the world has turned out. Defining what it takes to finish well provides a reminder we can use to keep ourselves on track.

As Steve Jobs said:

> "Remembering that I'll be dead soon is the most important tool I've ever encountered to help me make the big choices in life. Because almost everything – all external expectations, all pride, all fear of embarrassment or failure – these things just fall away in the face of death, leaving only what is truly important. Remembering that you are going to die is the best way I know to avoid the trap of thinking you have something to lose. You are already naked. There is no reason not to follow your heart."

Tool Four: Comparing Your Alternatives

In Chapter 3 you identified options for moving forward from among ten types of opportunity. You might already have decided which of these options you prefer. Or you might like to use the Morning Pages tool to think through your decision.

A more analytical approach is to choose your top alternatives, then compare their upsides and downsides, together with how easy each one would be to implement.

This tool can be used to aid your decision. Or it can be used to review and check a decision you have already made.

We can never know with 100 percent certainty how things are going to turn out. A good leader will shift to action with something between 40 and 80 percent confidence. Any earlier and you risk acting on too little information. Any later and you risk unnecessary delay. What is appropriate depends on you and the situation.

Think about your time frame: when do you need to take a decision by? How important is this issue compared with the other priorities you face? What resources are appropriate and available? Who are the key stakeholders? Which options will they support or resist? What are the key success factors? How quickly does your solution need to be put into place? How long does it need to last? What does this mean for the upsides and downsides of each of the ways forward you identified?

By rating each of your options for moving forward on upsides, downsides, and ease of implementation you can map them on the following chart:

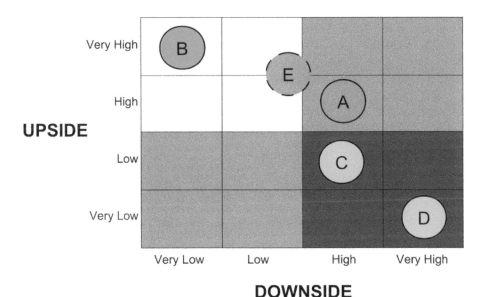

This example shows the alternatives I faced in deciding how to deal with my illness.

Option A was to take the treatment being offered. This had a high upside (of saving my life) but also serious potential downsides, the side-effects. This would be a medium-difficult path to follow, so on a 'traffic light' scale of red/amber/green it would be amber.

Option B was to find a surgeon who would give me the outcomes I wanted: very high upside with very low downside. This seemed the most difficult way forward, so I have coloured it red.

Option C was to change diet, exercise, and other factors in the hope of remission. My view was that this held a low chance of cure, with high probability of increased illness, but it was an easy route to take so I have coloured it green.

Option D represents the "do nothing" choice: easy to implement (green), with potentially very little upside and very high downside.

Option E, "Find out more information about alternative treatments," was no longer applicable by the time I made this chart so it is shown dotted. Earlier I had used it to investigate other options. Since my illness was slow moving I considered the downside risk was real but low and the upside potential was high to very high. And that is how it turned out.

Drawing this chart for some or all of the ten types of opportunity you identified in Chapter 3 will bring clarity on whether you are more interested in pursuing the highest upside (biggest opportunity) or the lowest downside (smallest risk). Do you prefer the easiest, quickest, or cheapest way forward? Or are you looking for a balanced mix?

There is no 'right' answer here. We all have to define our own priorities, let go of our 'shoulds' and other mis-blinks, and choose the mix of upsides, downsides, and effort that are right for us, given the situation.

Even if you take your decision in other ways, perhaps simply gut feel, this chart can still be useful to make the key factors behind that decision clearer. I, for example, did not use it in deciding how to proceed with my treatment. But I gained two valuable insights from drawing it after I had made my decision. One was the realisation that I had chosen what seemed like the most difficult way forward. Given that the outcome would affect the rest of my life it made sense to me to choose the highest potential upside, despite the difficulty. As Elon Musk puts it, "When something is important enough, you do it even if the odds are not in your favor."

The second insight, which came later, was that as soon as I had committed to what seemed like the hardest way forward, it turned out not to be so difficult at all: everything fell into place very easily.

Choosing the Best Opportunity for You

The time has come to make a decision: to choose which of the options you identified in Chapter 3 you are going to pursue. We know why this choice matters and we know why we can sometimes get stuck. We also know that we have the tools to get unstuck if we need to.

As you choose from among your options you might like to think of Travis Kalanick. When he became an employee at his first startup he didn't know that the firm was going to be sued for $250 billion. That is not a misprint. The company was sued for $250 billion. He kept going, resolved that situation, launched his own startup, led it through difficulties, sold it. Then he looked for new opportunities, chose the one that suited him best, and became cofounder and CEO of Uber. Being sued for $250 billion along the way didn't stop him and it needn't stop you either.

In a time of churning, all ways forward will be unpredictable. The only way to find out what is possible is to take action to make it happen. The best way to do that is to choose the way forward that will fuel and sustain you with the greatest levels of enthusiasm, joy, and inspiration. There is every reason to follow your heart.

No matter what then happens, you now have the tools to handle it: to centre and ground, make sense of the situation, find the opportunities, and choose whichever one will suit you best. The biggest risk is to do what Hamlet did, which was to not-choose.

In the case of my illness, what I found was that once I had chosen and committed to the best way forward for me, even though it seemed the most difficult, suddenly everything fell into place.

This well-known quote from Scottish climber WH Murray's book *The Scottish Himalayan Expedition* shows that other people have experienced this as well:

> "Concerning all acts of initiative (and creation), there is one elementary truth, the ignorance of which kills countless ideas and splendid plans: that the moment one definitely commits oneself, then Providence moves too. All sorts of things occur to help one that would never otherwise have occurred. A whole stream of events issues from the decision, raising in one's favour all manner of unforeseen incidents and meanings and material assistance, which no man could have dreamt would

have come his way. I learned a deep respect for one of Goethe's couplets:

'Whatever you can do or dream you can, begin it.
Boldness has genius, power and magic in it!' "

If you find yourself still hesitating over which opportunity is best for you, ask yourself what you don't like about the opportunities you have identified and what you want instead. Then revisit Chapter 3 with this in mind and look for new opportunities that have those characteristics.

Otherwise, apply whichever tools from this chapter seem most useful to you (as well as the others from Chapters 1-3). Be clear with yourself about what it will take for you to finish well. And then choose a next step that will take you in that direction, with an appropriate mix of upsides and downsides for where you are now.

The rest of *Inner Leadership* will prepare you to implement that choice.

Conclusions

This chapter has been about deciding which of the ten types of opportunity identified in Chapter 3 you want to pursue. If you have experienced any churning while reading it, remember to use the tools of Chapter 1 to centre and ground.

We are not just human beings, we are human becomings. The choices we make about how to move forward today will affect the person we become tomorrow. If we keep this in mind then we can turn the apparent crises we face into opportunities for self-actualisation: for becoming who we most want to be. We can take back control of our destiny, learning, growing, and achieving whatever is possible in the times we happen to have been born into.

When we call an event in our lives a crisis what we usually mean is that it is a situation that is taking us outside our ability to handle it as routine and is affecting us emotionally. What this, in turn, means is that we are *imagining* it means something about our competence, significance, or likeability.

But the story of the Taoist farmer shows that we can never know how a situation will turn out. And Chapter 3 showed that it is we who create our opportunities, from the ways we choose to respond to the situations we find ourselves in.

If we ground ourselves, make sense of the situation, and find the ten types of opportunity, then we can choose a way forward that is best for us now. Not necessarily ideal or perfect, but best for us now.

Three common reasons why people sometimes remain stuck even though they can see a way forward are overthinking, not knowing who they want to become, and fear. The tools in this and the earlier chapters enable us to overcome these blockages.

Defining what it will take for you to have lived a worthwhile life defines what 'success' looks like for you. The more you spend your time working towards these outcomes, the happier you will feel, the more successful you will be.

Steve Jobs said there's no reason not to follow your heart. This enabled him to fulfil his personal goal of making "a dent in the universe." Travis Kalanick showed that even huge obstacles can be skirted around. All we have to do is choose, and take whatever step is best for us now.

In a time of churning, all ways forward will be unpredictable. The only way to find out what is possible is to take action to make it happen.

Choosing what is best for us gives us the maximum energy and enthusiasm to make our chosen path happen. And what WH Murray, Goethe, and others have found is that once we definitely commit then Providence conspires to support us: our chosen way forward suddenly becomes easier than we imagined.

Chapter 6 will show us how to turn your chosen way forward into an inspiring vision. But first, in Chapter 5, we compare it against your purpose and values.

Measurement

Are you now clearer on the values you admire in other people, what they love that you love them for loving, the types of achievement you admire, and what you see as flaws in people?

Have you learned the lessons of a past decision? Do you now know what will it take for you to have lived a worthwhile life? Do you know what advice your 86-year-old self would give you now?

Have you chosen a direction to move forward in?

On a scale of 0 to 10, how able are you now to choose and pursue the best way forward for you? How does this compare with where you were at the start of the chapter?

What differences will this make in your life? What benefits will that bring? How valuable is that to you?

Is it a priority for you to strengthen these abilities further? Why? How much time will you allocate to achieving this?

Measuring Inner Leadership

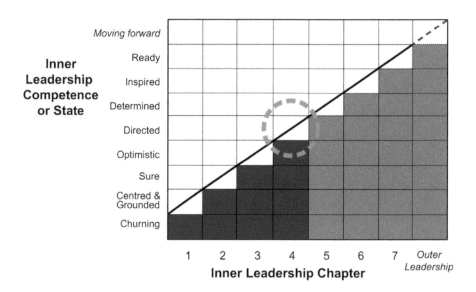

5. KNOW YOUR PURPOSE AND VALUES

To reach this point you have faced the churning, steadied yourself, and made sense of the situation. You have found the opportunities that exist in any 'crisis' and you have chosen the best way forward for you.

Before you shift to implementation there are three more steps to take. You need to describe your chosen way forward in a way that inspires you and other people to *want* to make it happen. You need to prepare for the inner challenges that will arise during implementation. And before you do either of those things, you need to define your purpose and values.

In a churning world, spending time to define your purpose and values might seem like a distraction from the urgent priorities we all face. But knowing these two things will bring you faster, clearer decision-making, plus better focus, motivation, flexibility, and results.

In a churning world, the one thing you can guarantee is that your vision and your journey towards it will not turn out the way you expected. So, as well as being clear about what your vision is and how to overcome the disruptions that will inevitably arise along the way, it is also important to define *why* you are making this journey and *how* you want to go about doing so.

That is what this chapter is about.

Before we begin, on a scale of 0 to 10, how clear are you now on what your purpose and values are?

Achieving Goals in Uncertain Times

Achieving your chosen way forward in a world that is churning requires a different set of skills from achieving the same goals in a stable environment. What are those skills and how can we acquire them?

Benchmarking is the process of looking for existing best practices in other industries, then adapting them to meet your needs. The best practice example of how to accomplish specific, measurable goals in highly uncertain, even hostile, environments must surely come from elite army units. Special forces operating behind enemy lines know that no plan survives contact with the enemy. Yet they manage to achieve their goals, despite these difficulties, by defining two things.

First, as well as knowing their primary objective (to capture the target, gather intelligence, or whatever) they also make sure that every team member understands the wider purpose of the mission: the role it plays in the larger campaign. Then, when things turn out differently from what was expected, they can easily adapt to carry out other actions in pursuit of the same aims and purpose.

Second, each unit is also given rules of engagement. These define what actions (such as returning fire) are allowed and not allowed under different circumstances. This keeps the unit focused on its highest priorities and maximises its chances of success. It also minimises the likelihood of unwanted outcomes.

By defining these two simple principles of conduct – purpose and rules of engagement – elite army units are able to go into highly unpredictable territory and adapt to changing circumstances in ways that maximise their potential to achieve the outcomes they seek. They become able to achieve the best that is possible, even under changing circumstances, without the need for everything to run exactly according to plan.

As we move forward to accomplish the objectives we chose in Chapter 4, we too will face unpredictable circumstances. Things will turn out differently from the ways we expected. People will behave differently from how we would have liked. And actions we take will have different outcomes from what we intended.

The equivalents of purpose and rules of engagement for us are our purpose and values. These define the underlying intent behind what we are doing and how we choose to behave under any circumstances. By getting clear on our purpose and values we give ourselves the focus and the flexibility to continue achieving the results that matter most, no matter what happens. And unlike the army units, we get to choose our purpose and values for ourselves.

Benefits of Knowing Your Purpose and Values

When everything is a priority, nothing is.

Spending time to define your purpose and values will bring you eight major benefits.

1. Better Results

The more clearly you have defined your purpose and values, the better you will be able to focus your resources on what matters and ignore what doesn't. Inner clarity leads to outer results.

2. More Motivation

People who know their purpose and values are more able to keep going in the face of obstacles and negative feedback. The clearer you are on what is important to you, the less other people's criticism or disapproval will matter. "This is what matters to me and this is how I choose to behave in the world, irrespective of whether anybody else agrees with me, approves of me, or tries to stop me."

Remember also from Chapter 4 that your destiny is a destination *"intended for a purpose."* Being clear on what that purpose is brings passion, joy, enthusiasm, and momentum to your journey.

3. Fewer Problems and Distractions

Winston Churchill said, "You will never reach your destination if you stop to throw stones at every dog that barks." If you know your purpose and values then each time an issue arises you can ask yourself whether it is relevant to your purpose and values. If it is then it is a priority for you. If it isn't then ignore it. It is someone else's fight.

Only when you know what matters can you ignore what doesn't.

4. Clearer Opportunities

As you move towards your vision many opportunities will arise. Do you have the time and resources to pursue them all?

Knowing your purpose and values will help you decide which are truly opportunities for you and which are distractions.

5. Clearer Outcomes

Once you have chosen to engage with an issue, your purpose and values provide a shorthand to quickly identify the outcomes you seek. What would the outcome look like if your purpose and values were being upheld?

Using purpose and values enables you to see more quickly *what* you want to create, which frees up more time and resources for working on *how* to achieve that.

6. A Greater Feeling of Control

In a world of constant churning everything can seem to be out of control. How can you expect to control anything unless you have the resources of a billionaire, a president, or a CEO? But when you become that billionaire, president, or CEO you find you have so much more at stake, and so many more issues to contend with, that you aren't really in control then either. Nobody is.

The only thing we can control is ourselves.

Knowing our purpose and values gives us a focus that enables us to choose our behaviour, choose what we engage with, and how. Then we can extend our reach and influence. This is true power.

In a churning world, where everything is unpredictable, the greatest degree of control we can hope to achieve is to work on an opportunity that inspires us, in line with our overall purpose and values. Achieving this is what *Inner Leadership* is all about.

7. Immediate Results

Peter Drucker said that success was not only about finishing but about finishing well. Your future vision has two parts: the results you will create and the culture you will live by once that vision is achieved.

By living according to the values of that culture now, you immediately achieve half of your vision. The tangible results you seek will then become easier to achieve as well.

8. More Freedom, Flexibility, and Adaptability

When the way forward or opportunity you have chosen is just one way of achieving your wider purpose then it becomes easier to adapt when events turn out differently from how you expected. You simply make sense of the new situation and find a new opportunity to pursue: one that is still in line with your purpose but fits better with the way events and reality have turned out. You recover more quickly from setbacks and become more flexible to changing circumstances.

When the world is churning it makes sense to expect that events will not turn out the way you expected. Knowing your purpose brings you continuity and stability in a changing world.

An Example: Steve Jobs on Purpose and Values

Is it really feasible to live in line with our purpose and values? What would happen if we did?

As part of his Stanford commencement address, Steve Jobs summed up the philosophy his life experience had taught him.

He didn't use the words 'purpose' or 'values'. Instead he talked about 'love', 'inner voice', 'heart', and 'intuition'.

He said:

"Your work is going to fill a large part of your life, and the only way to be truly satisfied is to do what you believe is great work. And the only way to do great work is to love what you do...

Your time is limited, so don't waste it living someone else's life. Don't be trapped by dogma – which is living with the results of other people's thinking. Don't let the noise of others' opinions drown out your own inner voice. And most important, have the courage to follow your heart and intuition. They somehow already know what you truly want to become. Everything else is secondary."

The best way I know to uncover what our love, inner voice, heart, and intuition are trying to tell us is to define our purpose and values. Then we can use them to consciously guide our decisions, and learn from experience as we move forward. The work of Chapters 1 to 4 has been useful preparation for this.

Tool One: Identify Your Purpose in Life

You might already know what your life's purpose is. If not, a quick search on the Internet will bring you literally millions of pages that talk about how to find it.

By far the best and simplest approach that I have found is the 'Life Purpose Exercise' offered by Jack Canfield® on his website (www.jackcanfield.com) and adapted from a tool originally developed by Arnold M. Patent in his book, *You Can Have It All*.

I like this approach because it involves answering just three straightforward questions and takes only about ten minutes to complete a first draft. Then you can try it out, see what happens, and develop it further over time.

My version of the four steps is as follows.

Step 1: Identify Your Two Best Qualities

What are the two best qualities you bring to the world?

If you find it difficult to pick only two you might ask a few trusted friends what qualities they see in you. Listen to their answers, ignore what you don't like, and keep what you do. Then pick, choose, or combine the rest to come up with the two qualities that *you* feel best describe you, that you most like about yourself: qualities that you love expressing and which summarise the essence of who you are.

For Jack Canfield the answers are love and joy.

I wasn't sure what qualities to pick for myself so I asked a good friend. She said the two qualities that best describe me are humanity and intelligence. I wasn't sure but I couldn't think of anything better. So I tried them out and they have lasted. Other people have qualities I cannot match, but these seem to encapsulate the way I approach life.

We all have special qualities that distinguish us from others. What are the two main qualities you bring to the world?

Step 2: Say How You Love Expressing Those Qualities

Next, ask yourself how you most love applying these qualities. When you are putting them into practice, what outcomes are you trying to create in the people around you? What's the change you're aiming to make in the world?

For Jack Canfield it's about creating inspiration and empowerment. He loves inspiring people with stories (like the *Chicken Soup* books), and empowering people (through his various training products and services).

For me, what I most enjoy is two things. First, I like seeing people achieve clarity about their current situation, where they want to get to, and how they are going to get there. Second, I love seeing them gain the energy and inspiration to shift into making that happen. Putting these two things together, what I love achieving when I express my two best qualities is to help people find the clarity and inspiration they need to move to action.

What outcomes do you love achieving when you are putting your best qualities into practice?

Step 3: Describe Your Ideal World

What would the world be like right now if it were perfect, according to you? What would you see, hear, feel, taste, or smell? What would that mean? What kind of a world is that?

For Jack Canfield it would be a world where everyone was living their highest vision. For me it would be a generative world.

What is 'generative'? Well, to me a generative world is generous and creative. It's a place where every person contributes the most to their organisation by most fully expressing their unique selves. Apple trees are generative: in the process of producing more apple trees they also provide pollen and nectar for bees, apples for us to eat, oxygen for animals to breathe, and so on. A generative world is a place where the more we become our best selves, the more we grow the size and health of the system as a whole. It is abundant, productive, dynamic, and evolving. It's a place where, at the end of each year, we have *more* of the key resources that matter, not fewer.

Ultimately, though, just as I don't really understand what Jack Canfield's 'highest vision' means to him, it doesn't really matter what 'generative' means to me. The point is for you to find a way of expressing *your* ideal world in a way that makes sense to *you*.

What would the world be like if it were perfect, according to you? What kind of a world is that?

Step 4: Put It All Together

To find your purpose in life, or a first draft that you can develop over time, take your three answers above and join them to form a sentence.
For example:

> "The purpose of my life is to use my [two main qualities] to [achieve what you said was the way you most love expressing those qualities], to create [your ideal world]."

For Jack Canfield this would be:

> "The purpose of my life is to use my love and joy to inspire and empower people, to create a world where everyone is living their highest vision."

He prefers to change the wording and say:

> "My life purpose is to inspire and empower people to live their highest vision in the context of love and joy, and for the highest good of all concerned."

My answer is:

> "The purpose of my life is to use my humanity and intelligence to help people find the clarity and inspiration that enables them to move to action to create a generative world."

or, perhaps better:

> "My purpose is to create a generative world, by using my humanity and intelligence to help people find the clarity and inspiration that enables them to take their best next step towards becoming whoever they most want to be."

Writing this book fits well with that.

In a changing economy, knowing our purpose makes it easier for us to choose new roles when we need to. And the more we select roles in line with our purpose, the more we are using our best qualities to create our ideal world and becoming our unique selves: self-actualising.

So combine the three elements of your purpose in different ways until you find a layout that resonates and has meaning for you.

Remember, there is no 'right answer' and nobody else needs to see this unless you want them to. The point is to draft something that feels right and try it out. Then update it and improve it over time.

Living on Purpose Is Good for You

In 2007, Professors John Cacioppo and Steve Cole discovered that the genes of people who felt lonely were altered in ways that reduced their ability to fight off viruses and increased their risks of inflammatory diseases such as cancer.

In 2010-13, Cole and psychologist Barbara Fredrickson looked for the opposite effect: they studied the genes of people living highly connected, hedonistic lives, as well as those of people who lived lives built around purpose. What they found was that the hedonistic lifestyles had no measurable effect on genes. But the genes of people who lived purposeful lives showed improved antiviral response and reduced risk of inflammatory diseases. Three larger studies since then have shown similar results.

This genetic effect implies that purpose is connected with evolution, but that's a story for another day. Living in line with your purpose not only makes you freer and more focused, it also changes the way your genes express themselves, making you healthier and enabling you to live longer.

Tool Two: Find Your Values

I like this method for finding your values because it is based on the direct reality of your own experience.

The technique is this. Think back to times in your life when you felt fully absorbed in your work. You lost track of time, felt fully alive, in flow, operating at your maximum potential, doing what you are here to do. Find between one and three occasions.

For each situation, ask yourself what values were you upholding in that moment when you felt most alive. What values were you standing up for, taking action in support of? There might be more than one. Write them all down.

If you find it difficult to identify the values you were standing *for*, try thinking of situations where you stood up *against* something. What were you were standing against? What values are the opposite of that?

Working on this exercise with a trusted friend who asks open questions can help you to tease out and clarify your thinking: "Why? What do you mean? Can you give an example?" It will take probably about 10 to 15 minutes for each person to complete the exercise.

You can also add your answers from the first tool in Chapter 4. These are the values you admired in others, what you loved them for loving, the opposites of their flaws, and the things you admired them for achieving. All these are also indicators of your values. Adding them will give you a deeper, more nuanced understanding and more confidence in your final result.

You now almost certainly have a list of more than three values. Group, merge, and combine them until you have distilled them down to find your three core values.

For example, I remembered times when I felt most alive while giving talks and presentations, and once there was time when I lost track of time while working on a spreadsheet(!). The underlying values I identified myself as standing up for during those moments included truth, fairness, respect, and being fact-driven. For me, I realised, these were all different aspects of a deeper value: integrity.

Following a similar process, I came up with three more values – harmony, empowerment, and action orientation – but I couldn't see how to get the total down to three. Then I realised that, for me, integrity combined with action equals honour: honour is integrity put into action. This might not make sense according to some dictionary definitions but that doesn't matter. This exercise is not about dictionaries. It is about finding the words that best describe the times when you have felt most fully alive, in flow, doing what you are here to do. Use whatever words feel right to you.

The more you put into this activity now the more confident you will be of the results you obtain and the more useful they will be. For me, the process took a couple of hours and an overnight sleep before I finally decided on my three values. But the answers I came up with have lasted ever since. My values are honour, harmony, and empowerment. I feel most solidly grounded, joyful, and alive when I am working and acting in alignment with them.

What are the three core values you stand for?

Complete at least a first draft of your purpose and values before continuing.

Applying this New Information

Once you have defined your purpose and values your first reaction will probably be to realise that you don't always live up to them. This is to be expected. We are all human beings, not saints, and many of us live in circumstances that are less than ideal. So give your purpose and values a chance to settle while you get used to them.

Abraham Maslow showed us that human beings all have a hierarchy of needs. The lower levels are things like air and water, food and shelter, love, belonging, and esteem. The top level is called self-actualisation. Your purpose and values show you what self-actualisation looks like for you. Living in line with your purpose and values defines what 'success' looks like for you.

As with all strategic goals, achieving this doesn't happen overnight. But no matter where you are starting from, your purpose and your values provide a beacon for you to move towards, even if your environment is not completely supportive.

As the example of Karim Wasfi on page 139 shows, there is always something we can do in line with our purpose and values. And when we use our values as a focus for taking even small actions, we get to create our ideal world, in ways that rekindle the feelings of joy, flow, and aliveness that our chosen values represent.

We also get to experience the eight benefits listed earlier, including resilience, flexibility, and a sense of continuity and control.

On a scale of 0 to 10, how fully would you say that you are living your purpose and values today? What would your life be like if your answer was 10?

Where are the major areas of alignment today? What are the major areas of non-alignment? Where would it be easiest to make a change?

Now let's test your purpose and values.

Think back to the option for moving forward that you chose in Chapter 4. Does pursuing that opportunity help to achieve your purpose? Is it in line with your values? (If not, do you want to revise your purpose and values; or revisit Chapter 4 and choose a different option for moving forward?) If it fits, is this your current best opportunity for moving forward towards self-actualisation, the best mix of upsides and downsides for where you are now?

Inner leadership, like life, is an iterative process. Sailors often change direction back and forth against the wind but that doesn't alter the ultimate destination they are heading for. New insights lead us to new actions, which lead to new insights, and new actions. The direction you chose in Chapter 4 is an opportunity for you to bring your purpose and values alive in the world. If you repeat this cycle over time, working on whatever most inspires you next and creating the new results you now care most about, you become unstoppable.

This chapter has added another layer of emotional engagement to the inspiration that inner leadership is all about. The next step is to build on this further, by learning to describe the opportunity you chose in Chapter 4 as an inspiring vision.

Conclusions

This chapter has been about identifying two elements that are key to staying motivated and directed during times of change. If you have experienced any churning while reading it remember to use the tools of Chapter 1 to centre and ground.

Elite army units provide a best practice example of how to remain focused yet flexible in highly unpredictable environments. They achieve this by being clear on the wider purpose of their mission and by defining clear rules of engagement.

Defining our purpose and values brings us benefits that include faster, clearer decision-making, and better focus, motivation, adaptability, and results.

Living in line with your purpose is a way to apply your best qualities in the way you most enjoy, and to build your ideal world.

Living in line with your values is a way to feel more fully alive, in flow, operating at your full potential, doing what you are here to do.

In a churning world it might not be possible to achieve this 100% of the time. But once you know your purpose and values then you become more able to choose your responses and also experience more energy, enthusiasm, and resilience.

In a changing world, purpose and values bring us continuity, stability, and determination.

In the next chapter we will see how to use your purpose and values to build an inspiring vision of the opportunity you chose to pursue in Chapter 4.

Measurement

On a scale of 0 to 10, how clear are you now on what your purpose and values are? How does this compare with where you were at the start of the chapter?

What differences will this make in your life? What benefits will that bring? How valuable is that to you?

Is it a priority for you to strengthen these abilities further? Why? How much time will you allocate to achieving this?

(Record your answers in whatever workbook or notebook you are using.)

Measuring Inner Leadership

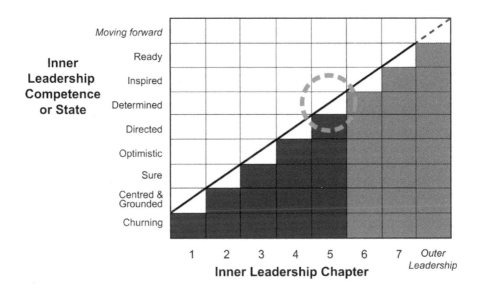

6. CREATE AN INSPIRING VISION

Vision matters. It makes us come alive.

So far we've focused on using the skills of inner leadership to develop inspiration and emotional engagement in ourselves. We've learned to steady ourselves, make sense of our situations, and choose the opportunity or way forward that is best for us. As we work to make that choice a reality in a churning world, we've seen how knowing our purpose and values will bring us greater focus, flexibility, energy, and enthusiasm.

Now we need to convince other people to support our project: as customers, colleagues, investors, and in other roles. The best way to do that is by inspiring them.

This chapter describes seven building blocks that you can use to describe your chosen opportunity as an inspiring vision.

Before we begin, on a scale of 0 to 10, how able are you currently to describe your chosen way forward in ways that inspire you and other people to want to make it happen?

Three Benefits of Inspiration

Whichever way forward you have chosen, you will only succeed if you convince other people to stop doing things the way they do them today and start doing what you are suggesting instead. The best way to achieve that is by inspiring them. Because, as Steve Jobs put it, "If you are working on something exciting that you really care about, you don't have to be pushed. The vision pulls you."

Building inspiration in the people around you will benefit you not just once but three times.

First, in a time of churning, people are likely to be experiencing uncertainty and confusion. Getting them to switch to the direction you are proposing means overcoming their inertia, doubt, and even fear. The best way to achieve that is by providing a large helping of vision, inspiration, and emotional engagement.

Second, once people have joined your project, the next thing that will happen is that difficulties will arise. In a time of churning this is inevitable. But the more emotional engagement these people feel, the more they will be able to overcome or work around these difficulties without needing further input from you. This applies no matter what their role is: the more inspiration that customers, employees, and investors get from participating in your project, the more they will continue to engage with it, no matter what difficulties arise. A recent (2016) survey of tech companies, for example, showed that employees at Tesla and SpaceX had the most stressful and the lowest paying jobs. But their roles were also the most meaningful and inspiring.

Third, over time the level of engagement felt by your team will show up in the results you produce together. Research by Gallup found that companies with highly emotionally engaged workforces "outperform their peers by 147% in earnings per share... A highly engaged workforce means the difference between a company that outperforms its competitors and one that fails to grow." The more inspired your team remains over time, the more advantage your project will have.

Building inspiration and emotional engagement will spur people to join your project. It will motivate them to stick with it. And it will increase the levels of contribution they make while they are with you. It's also more enjoyable to be around.

And what other 'technology' do you know that can deliver a 147% improvement in earnings per share?

The question then arises, how can we achieve this?

The answer is by building an inspiring vision of your project. Or rather, by telling an inspiring, visionary story about it.

Seven Building Blocks of An Inspiring Vision

There is no fixed template for what it takes to create an inspiring vision. No two inspiring leaders are the same. But just as every great painting is formed from the same basic colours, and every great piece of music is formed from the same basic notes, so every great vision is formed from the same basic building blocks, combined and arranged in different ways.

There are seven building blocks that you can use to create an inspiring vision of the way forward you have chosen. Three of them are general, to do with style and approach, and four are specific to the particular way forward you have chosen. Which blocks you use, how you combine them, and how you bring them alive is up to you.

Building Block 1:
Speak with Your Own Authentic Voice

The first building block is to speak with your own authentic voice. This is partly because the story you tell must be one that inspires you, and if it inspires you then it will inspire other people. And partly it is because your own authentic voice is the only one you will be able to maintain consistently as you move forward.

More than this, speaking with your own authentic voice is the right thing to do because the direction you have chosen is the one that matters most to you. It is the direction that aligns best with what you most want to achieve in your life, and with who you most want to become. If you share that authentically with people then they will hear it, not just in what you say but in how you say it. Your words will resonate with those who share similar or overlapping goals and ambitions, and you will attract to you the people you want most: the people who will join you for the long haul. Your tribe.

Even if there are difficulties, it is better to acknowledge these authentically up front and to show how they don't matter in the light of something more important. Four hundred years ago, for example, a country came under threat from invasion. The ruler at the time was a woman in a man's world. Many of her own people thought she was not up to the job, simply because of her sex. Attempts had been made to kill her. With threats coming from home and abroad, Queen Elizabeth I might simply have run away. Or she could have bluffed it out: "Everything will be fine." Instead, she faced the situation full on and explicitly addressed what she knew many people were thinking. In a speech to her assembled army she spoke what became her most famous words: "I know I have the body of a weak, feeble woman," she said, "but I have the heart and stomach of a king, and of a king of England too."

Her authenticity and determination won her audience over. And once they had decided to listen to her, they then listened to what she had to say. Then they did what needed to be done.

So, create a vision first of all that is true to you, that matters to you and inspires you. Don't include anything in it just because it is on this list of building blocks. And don't leave anything out that you think matters, just because it doesn't seem to be on the list.

Your vision will become most inspiring when it comes authentically from you.

Building Block 2:
Make It Relevant for Your Audience

The second building block is about taking the inspiration you feel and converting it into something your audience will not only relate to but will adopt as their own. As Henry Ford put it, "Nobody at work is apathetic except those who are in pursuit of someone else's objective."

This building block is not simply about describing the issues your audience cares about (the "What's in it for me?") or appealing to the principles and values they believe in. This building block is about embracing your audience's language and worldview. It is about plugging in to the way they experience the world, and shifting that to where you want it to be, using a mix of logic and emotion that works for them.

The best politicians understand this need to engage differently with different groups of people. Because the better they do this, the better each constituency buys into the vision and makes it their own.

So empathise with your audience. Put yourself in their shoes. What are they thinking about? What are they feeling? What are their hopes, fears, and priorities? Where do they want to get to?

Do they want a challenge? Do they want to feel heroic? Do they want to stretch and grow and feel the sense of accomplishment that comes from achieving something difficult and worthwhile? Or are they feeling so afraid that they find it difficult to see the opportunities in the situation? Do they simply want to feel safe?

The later building blocks will enable you to highlight the need for action, the opportunity to create something worthwhile, and the steps that are needed to get there. But none of this will happen unless you can structure and communicate it in a way that makes sense to the audience you are talking to and meshes with the reality they are experiencing now.

Metaphor can be a good way to help people reframe the way they see a situation. When the process of obtaining democracy in Burma was moving too slowly, many people wanted to switch to taking direct action. Democracy campaigner and Nobel Peace Prize winner Aung San Suu Kyi used metaphor to convince them to maintain a non-violent approach. "If you look at the democratic process as a game of chess," she said, "there have to be many, many moves before you get to checkmate. And simply because you do not make any checkmate in three moves does not mean it's stalemate... This is what the democratic process is like."

Her method of generating support was to be calm, still, and consistent: to lead by steadfast if undramatic example, and nevertheless to remain visionary and inspiring. Getting people to reframe the way they think about a situation will lead them to take different actions.

Some companies are applying this approach to make their mission statements more relevant to one key audience, their customers. Nike, for example, expresses its mission not as "To be the global leader in the sporting goods industry" but "To bring inspiration and innovation to every athlete* in the world. (*If you have a body, you are an athlete.)" Starbucks sees its mission not as "To sell the best coffee in the world" but "To inspire and nurture the human spirit – one person, one cup, and one neighborhood at a time."

These reframings certainly look like attempts to make the firms' stories more relevant to their customers' world views. But whether they translate into improved results will depend on how well these words are received not only by customers, but also by other audiences, such as employees.

That, in turn, will depend on whether the rhetoric is translated into new actions, attitudes, and behaviours by the firms. And this brings us to the two final ways in which you can achieve this building block: your body language and the way you dress.

When Elizabeth I was facing her ultimate threats, from home and abroad, she did two things that communicated her message without saying a word. First, she dressed in armour, unheard of for a woman. Then she left behind her company of bodyguards and rode slowly through a dangerous mass of several thousand heavily armed soldiers with an escort of just four men and two page boys. Eyewitnesses said she rode "like some Amazonian empress… full of princely resolution."

Without speaking a word she demonstrated that she was not afraid of the threat from home, and that she had the strength and determination to counter the threat from abroad. Her audience saw that and responded.

Your audience will not remember everything you tell them but they will remember how you make them feel. This building block is about shaping those feelings.

Building Block 3:
Let People Make Up Their Own Minds But Make Sure They Choose

As well as articulating your vision in a way that is authentic to you and memorable for your audience, it is also important to remember the reason why you are sharing this vision. You want people to make a decision. And you want them to change their behaviour in support of your project.

To achieve these outcomes it might seem to make sense to push as hard as you can to get people to join you. But in a churning world difficulties are bound to arise. If you have pushed people into joining you, rather than letting them make up their own minds, then every time an issue arises you will have to convince them all over again.

The CEOs of Unilever and Apple both know this. In recent years both have effectively said to shareholders, "This is where we are going. If you don't like it, get out of the stock." They are sure of their direction and they know that investors who are not committed to travelling the same path will be a drain on their time and energy. In a churning world, this is time and energy they do not have to spare.

The same applies to your employees, customers, and anybody else you want to support your project. Nobody can tell another person what to do. And no matter what they say to your face, each person will make up their own mind eventually anyway.

The more you can inspire people to choose, for their own reasons, to travel with you through an imperfect world, the more you will build a team that actively works to find the opportunities in each problem that arises, rather than questioning every step of the journey. They will do this because in helping you to achieve your purpose they will also be helping themselves to achieve theirs.

All you can do is two things. Use the other six building blocks to build a vision-story that is inspiring enough for people to make it their own. And then make sure they choose: are they 'on the bus' or 'off the bus'? Do they want to lead, follow, or get out of the way?

Once you have the right people on your team, then you can decide where you want to drive the 'bus' together, and how quickly.

From General to Specific

These first three building blocks have covered the general aspects of your vision-story, its style and approach. The remaining four are specific to the particular direction you have chosen to travel, the opportunity you have decided to pursue.

Research has shown that successful strategic change happens when leaders combine three key elements: a clear definition of the problem, a clear definition of the alternative future they want to create, and clearly defined first steps to get there. Not the entire journey, just the first steps.

If any one of these factors is missing, the net result will be zero, so we can illustrate this as a formula by multiplying the three factors together:

$$\text{Successful Change} = \text{Clear Problem} \times \text{Clear Alternative} \times \text{Clear First Steps}$$

If you don't like maths, don't worry: the point here is simply that all three elements are necessary and required.

The remaining task of your vision-story is to bring these three essential features alive for your audience. We start by describing the problem.

Building Block 4:
Show There Is a Problem

If there's no problem there's no need to change. The difficulties of the current situation provide a large part of the motivation people will need to shift to doing something different. So be very clear about what that situation is and why they need to change. As Jack Welch used to say, when he was CEO of General Electric, "Face reality as it is, not as it was, or as you wish it to be."

The work you did in Chapters 2 and 3 can be invaluable here. Use Chapter 2 to bring your audience a clear understanding of the situation. Focus on the issues that matter most to them and the mindsets they will be applying. Remember that your goal is not so much to change the beliefs they have about the world as to change the actions they will take. Use your work in Chapter 3 to help them understand where the alternative responses they might be considering would lead to.

Remember the three blockages of Chapter 4, and don't over explain. You want to avoid analysis paralysis or overcoming your audience with fear. Make sure you deliver this building block in a way that shows them you are on their side (Block 2).

The more clearly you can show your audience that they have a problem they need to address, the keener they will be to find a solution.

Building Block 5:
Define the Future State You Want to Create

"A leader," Napoleon said, "is a dealer in hope." Having shown your audience why they need to change, your goal with this building block is to bring them that hope.

In one way, this is the easiest building block to address. You know the direction you want to take, and you know why it makes sense to you. You know what finished looks like, and you know what it means to finish well.

But how do you articulate all this in a way that will inspire other people?

In terms of Chapter 4 this is about showing them who they want to become, so the usual way to create hope is to describe a future that people can aspire and look forward to. Famously, Martin Luther King said "I have a dream... I have a dream... I have a dream..." He did not say, "I have a problem I need to be solved."

But you can also inspire people by describing a future that is filled with toil and struggle. In the bleak beginnings of World War Two, Winston Churchill needed his people to keep going. Inspiration for them at that stage came from the thought of not giving up: "We shall fight on the beaches, we shall fight on the landing grounds, we shall fight in the fields and in the streets... We shall never surrender."

Both approaches worked. Both were appropriate for their time. And both speakers used repetition for effect.

Another way to create a clear vision of the future is to set out a specific, measurable, achievable, realistic, and time-bound goal. This is what John F Kennedy did when he announced America's intention to go to the moon: "I believe that this nation should commit itself to achieving the goal, before this decade is out, of landing a man on the Moon and returning him safely to the Earth."

Alternatively, you could state your direction vaguely and metaphorically. Donald Trump became president by inspiring people with the vision that he would "Make America great again." Moses promised to lead his people to "a land flowing with milk and honey." And despite this lack of precision, or perhaps because of it, his audience followed him through the wilderness for 40 years.

Defining what you are going to create also implies defining when you are going to create it. Will you inspire people more by getting them to think about short-term results or the impacts in some far distant future?

One classic, short-term, approach is to define "What's in it for me?" for your audience. You might tell them, "Follow my plan and you'll make twice as much money next year as you did last." Following this approach, Kennedy could have argued that the space programme was the right thing to do because of the technological spin-offs it would bring, or the benefits to the economy. But he didn't do that.

Once short-term goals have been achieved, motivation can flag. People can feel more inspired for longer if you ask them to imagine a distant future. For Elon Musk, that future for humanity runs in one of two directions: "Either it's going to become multi-planetary," he says, "or it's going to remain confined to one planet and eventually there's going to be an extinction event." He formed SpaceX as a way to enable people to live on other planets. He inspires people to work for him by describing a long-term purpose.

Will you inspire your audiences more if you talk about laying bricks or about building a cathedral? Today or for the next 100 years?

There is no single right way to define the future state you want to create or the 'hope' Napoleon tells you to bring your audience. There is only what works for you and them, now.

Building Block 6:
Relate Your Message to Higher Principles, Values, Or Ideals

As well as telling your audience what you want to create, another way to inspire them is by telling them why it matters.

For John F Kennedy, the reason for going to the Moon was clear. "We choose to go to the Moon in this decade and do the other things not because they are easy, but because they are hard, because that goal will serve to organize and measure the best of our energies and skills."

Convincing your audience of why a vision matters is part of building the clarity and inspiration that sets events in motion.

What triggered the Boston Tea Party was a disagreement over tax. But what sustained America's War of Independence was the underlying principle of whether Great Britain had the right to tax its colonies. And it was principles, and not tax rates, that were enshrined in the eventual *Declaration of Independence*: "We hold these truths to be self-evident, that all men are created equal, that they are endowed by their Creator with certain unalienable Rights… That whenever any Form of Government becomes destructive of these ends, it is the Right of the People to alter or to abolish it."

It was principles (of liberty, equality, fraternity) that inspired the French Revolution. And it was principles ("no person may be held indefinitely without trial") that led Britain's barons to stand up against their king and demand the new laws of *Magna Carta*.

People take action to uphold principles.

I once took a flight with a BP executive who told me that the company's management had been astonished by the positive impact that their *Beyond Petroleum* rebranding initiative had had on the morale, energy, and enthusiasm of their people. Clearly (given the Deepwater Horizon explosion in the Gulf of Mexico) that direction was not sustained. But the opportunity was there, even if it was not fully grasped.

Being clear on the principles that explain why the vision matters is probably the one key feature missing from most corporate visions today. It is also the one key addition that would make the most difference to inspiration and performance.

So why does your vision matter? Why should I care? Who or what is it for? What are the purpose and values you defined in Chapter 5? How will following your vision contribute to what it means for me to live a worthwhile life? How will it help me to become the 86-year-old person I want to be? What are the purpose and values that will bring your audience a beacon of stability in a churning world?

If you can articulate all this, in ways that make sense to your different audiences, then they will help you to build your vision and fulfil your purpose, because in doing so they will be building and fulfilling their own purpose and values.

Building Block 7:
Define the Needed Steps and Show that They Are Achievable

Having shown your audience that they have a problem and painted an inspiring vision of what they could have instead, the one remaining question in their minds is likely to be whether or not they can achieve it. The goal of this building block is to show them that they can.

In 1944, General George Patton used this block repeatedly as he sought to motivate the inexperienced Third Army to follow up on the largest seaborne invasion in history. His task is not especially relevant to anything you or I will ever be called upon to undertake. But its scale is far greater and, in achieving it successfully, Patton gave us a fine example of how to apply Building Block 7. Many people consider the words he spoke to be one of the greatest motivational speeches of all time.

Patton wanted to inspire a group of people to do something daunting and huge that they had never done before. He achieved this by defining the steps that were needed and showing that they were achievable. He did this on three levels.

He reminded his team of the general behaviours he expected, such as "constant alertness" and "instant obedience."

He told them stories that gave specific examples of the kinds of actions they would be called upon to perform and reminded them that others before them had already done similar things: "You should have seen the trucks on the road to Gabès. Those drivers were magnificent. All day and all night they crawled along those son-of-a-bitch roads, never stopping, never deviating from their course with shells bursting all around them. Many of the men drove over 40 consecutive hours."

And he reassured his people emotionally that the role of each one of them was important and they wouldn't be alone: "An army is a team," he said. "It lives, eats, sleeps, and fights as a team. This individual hero stuff is bullshit."

The language Patton used might not be appropriate for your audience, but it was entirely appropriate for his and for the task he was calling on them to undertake. It was the language of the barracks and he delivered it in a humorous tone, piling example upon example upon example.

If you look back to Chapter 4, you will see that what he was also doing was motivating his people by telling them that they were significant, competent, and loved. These are the three core elements of our identities and Patton made sure he reinforced them in his team.

Kennedy approached this building block differently. Announcing the ten-year plan to put an astronaut on the moon, he defined only the high-level resources that would be assigned: "During the next five years the National Aeronautics and Space Administration expects to double the number of scientists and engineers in this area; to increase its outlays for salaries and expenses to $60 million a year; to invest some $200 million in plant and laboratory facilities…"

And as a third example, Tim Cook showed the importance of this building block in an interview he gave soon after his appointment as CEO of Apple. Describing his vision for the company, Cook focused almost entirely on the attitudes and behaviours that would enable the organisation to succeed. Here's what he said, with emphasis added:

"We believe that we are on the face of the earth **to make great products** and that's not changing. We are constantly focusing on **innovating**. We believe in the **simple not** the **complex**. We believe that we need to **own and control the primary technologies** behind the products that we make, and participate only in **markets where we can make a significant contribution**. We believe in **saying no to thousands** of projects, so that we can really **focus on the few** that are truly important and meaningful to us. We believe in **deep collaboration** and **cross-pollination** of our groups, which allow us to **innovate** in a way that others cannot. And frankly, we don't settle for anything less than **excellence** in every group in the company, and we have the **self-honesty** to admit when we're wrong and the **courage** to change. And I think regardless of who is in what job those **values** are so embedded in this company that Apple will do extremely well."

Cook knows that in a churning world he cannot lay out every step of the way. Instead he defines the company's purpose (to make great products) and its values (courage, excellence, and self-honesty). As we know, these will give Apple focus and flexibility in a changing world.

Then Cook describes a vision of the steps that will enable the company to bring its purpose and values to life: simplicity, control of primary technologies, focus (on projects and markets), and innovation ("in a way that others cannot") through deep collaboration and cross-pollination. These attitudes and behaviours are internal rather than external but they are still part of Building Block 7. And, as Cook says, achieving them will enable Apple to succeed in a churning world, no matter who is in what job.

To summarise, this building block can be about defining the steps, actions, activities, resources, attitudes, behaviours, competencies, and indeed emotional capacities needed to achieve your objective. They might be just the initial steps, or activities that continue and build over time.

Defining this block well is what gives your audience confidence to take the first step.

Putting the Blocks Together

In a moment you will take the seven building blocks and see how each applies to your situation. Then you will select the most relevant blocks and combine them. The best way to do this is by telling stories that will inspire your audience to support you.

Human beings are hard-wired for stories. We connect with them, engage with them, and remember them in ways that simply don't happen when we receive the same information in other forms. Princeton neuroscientist, Uri Hasson, has found that, "Story is the only

---

Learning From Leaders You Admire

Another way to develop an inspiring vision is to copy leaders you admire.

Think of a leader you admire and a time when they said or did something that inspired you.

What did you find most inspiring about what they said or did and the way they said or did it? These are the elements that are most likely to match your style.

Which of the seven building blocks do these elements relate or correspond to?

Is there anything the leader said or did that doesn't seem to fit into the seven building blocks? (Please let me know.)

How can you adapt what you find most inspirational in other leaders to create new inspiration in your current situation?

---

way to activate parts in the brain so that a listener turns the story into their own idea and experience."

More than this, when facts and emotions are combined into a story they create meaning. This is why we love movies. As screenwriting guru Robert McKee explains, "When an idea wraps itself around an emotional charge, it becomes all the more powerful, all the more profound, all the more memorable... In short, a story well told gives you the very thing you cannot get from life: meaningful emotional experience."

Story is the best way to deliver a vision that your audience will not only understand, but will find so meaningful and inspiring that they adopt it as their own. Told and retold by your team, a good story can then evolve as you move forward together and adapt to changing circumstances.

See what happens now if we improvise a deliberately bland sentence for each of the seven building blocks, but then join them to form a simple story:

"We are facing a difficult situation. It is unlike anything we have experienced before, but we come from a long line of people who have faced difficult situations and overcome them. We can't stay as we are, or go back to where we were: we have to move forward. If we go in the direction I am suggesting then we have the opportunity to build something special together. By following this path we will uphold the very principles we stand for. We already have all the tools and resources we need. The only question is, are you willing to step up now and play your part for the good of those who will come after you?"

Each building block on its own provides a single boring ingredient. Combined in the right order and proportions, they become a whole that is greater than the sum of its parts.

Imagine how much greater that effect will be when you vividly express each of your relevant building blocks and join them to tell your vision-story.

As Muhammad Ali said, "If my mind can conceive it, and my heart can believe it, then I can achieve it."

Story is the best way to combine fact and emotion so that you and other people will want to make your chosen way forward happen.

Tool One: Create Your Inspiring Vision

To create an inspiring vision-story for the opportunity you selected in Chapter 4, first make a prioritised list of the audiences you want to inspire. Put yourself at the top of the list.

Then for each audience, starting with yourself, work through the following six steps:

1. Make bullet point notes on how each building block might apply to your situation and this audience. (Writing your answers on post-it notes can be useful in the later steps.) Capture anything that comes to mind.
2. If a building block seems to be irrelevant, leave it out and move on. (You might ask yourself for clarity on why it doesn't apply.)
3. Include any new building blocks you identified from the 'Learning From Leaders You Admire' box. Add bullet point notes on how these might apply to your situation.
4. Review all the bullet points and group those that seem to go together. (Using post-it notes can be useful for this step.) Get a sense of the emerging story. Identify the points or themes that seem to stand out as most important.

5. Pull out these bullet points into a new, separate list. Group them into short phrases or sentences. Then arrange them in an order that seems to tell the story you want to tell to this audience. (Again, moving the post-it notes around can be a useful way to experiment.)

6. Develop your vision-story further. Flesh out the details. Try it out with your chosen audience. Learn and repeat.

The relevance of each building block will depend on the audience you are talking to, the level of engagement they already have, and the stage your project has reached. Don't try to include everything. What you leave out makes the story clearer. The seven blocks are a tool for quickly finding the elements of story that will resonate with this particular audience, now.

Experiment with putting your ideas in different orders. Find your voice. Find what works to engage, keep, and inspire your audience. Remember that in order to inspire others you first have to inspire yourself. (Morning Pages might be a useful way to think this through.)

If you find any of the building blocks difficult, revisit the other chapters. Taking the blocks in order, Chapter 1 can support you to connect more deeply with your authentic self. Chapter 7 provides ways to understand and connect with your audience more deeply. Chapter 4 covered making the decision to move forward. Chapters 2 and 3 were about understanding the current situation and how to deal with it. Chapter 4 is also about defining what you want to build. And Chapter 5 defines the principles that matter to you. Chapter 7 is about preparing for the first steps. Added to this, you know that *Inner Leadership* as a whole gives you the flexibility to be able to adapt and respond to whatever might happen next, which can be another important confidence-builder for taking the first step.

Experiment, improve, and don't expect instant results. In the months leading up to D-Day, General Patton improved his speech each time he delivered it to a different unit. Martin Luther King's famous "I have a dream" speech was improvised on the day, combining elements from earlier speeches. This immediacy is part of what makes it so powerful.

People will not remember the specific details of everything you tell them, but they will remember how you make them feel. So know your own truth and speak it authentically. Describe the vision-story that inspires you and then get others to buy into that as well.

Conclusions

If you have experienced any churning while reading this chapter, remember to use the tools of Chapter 1 to centre and ground.

This chapter has been about creating a vision that will act both as a call to action and a focus for that action.

As the writer and aviator Antoine de Saint Exupéry is often quoted as saying:

> "If you want to build a ship, don't drum up people to collect wood, and don't assign them tasks and work, but rather teach them to long for the endless immensity of the sea."

Vision gives people the energy they need to join your project and then stick with it when difficulties arise. Vision increases the level of contribution they make while they are with you, and it generates enthusiasm that is enjoyable to be around!

The best way to create an inspiring vision is by building a story. This creates something that your audience will not only understand but will find meaningful enough to adopt as their own. And as they tell and retell your story in their own words, so it will adapt and evolve as you move forward together.

Like any good story, your vision needs a beginning, a middle, and an end.

The beginning is a description of where you are now and why change is needed. The end is the outcome you want to create. The middle is a description of why this is the right path to take, and a clear definition of what the achievable first steps are.

The more you express your vision-story in terms that are relevant to your audience, the more sense it will make to them. The more authentically you deliver it, the more likely you are to attract to you the kinds of people you most want with you on your journey.

Finally, you need to ask your audience to make a choice. Are they with you or not? You cannot make this decision for them. You can only give them the information *they* need, in the form *they* need it, so that they can make a strong choice for themselves. The better you are able to inspire them to do this, the further and faster you will be able to move forward together.

People will not remember everything you tell them but they will remember how you make them feel. So know your truth, and speak it authentically and inspiringly. Describe the outcome that inspires you and get others to buy into that as well.

Once you have translated your chosen direction into a vision that inspires and engages people to travel with you, the next step is to prepare for implementation. This is what we shall do in Chapter 7.

Measurement

On a scale of 0 to 10, how able are you now to describe your chosen way forward as an inspiring vision? How does this compare with where you were at the start of the chapter?

What differences will this make in your life? What benefits will that bring? How valuable is that to you?

Is it a priority for you to develop your vision further before you start to share it with your target audience(s)? Why? How much time will you allocate to achieving this?

Measuring Inner Leadership

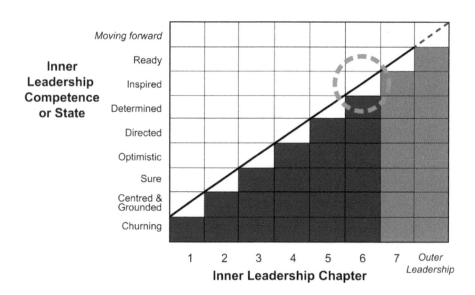

7. PREPARE FOR THE JOURNEY

As you work towards the objective you chose in Chapter 4, challenges will arise. This chapter is about preparing for those challenges, so that you maintain your levels of emotional engagement and enthusiasm as you go forward. It accomplishes this in two ways.

First, it describes the three phases of psychological and emotional transitions that you and your team will go through as you work towards your goal. It explains how to manage your way through the three stages and how to turn them to your advantage.

Second, it provides a map of *Inner Leadership*: a chart that you can use to guide you as you enter this new territory.

Before we begin, on a scale of 0 to 10, how well-prepared are you now to maintain your inspiration and that of your team as you move forward together towards the destination you chose in Chapter 4?

Three Phases of Transition

Whenever we start out on a new project, job, or relationship, our role and hence our identity changes. As we know from Chapter 4, changing identity can be difficult. So at the same time as you and your team are working together to build your new vision, you also need to be managing the inner psychological transitions you will all be going through. For some people these transitions will be large, for others small. But no matter what their size, they all matter. Because, as change management guru William Bridges puts it, "It isn't the changes that do you in, it's the transitions."

Changes are about what we do and how we do them. They are about events, things, places, and hierarchies. Changes are external, visible, and physical. They can happen quickly and are usually controllable and predictable.

Transitions are about who we are and how we feel. They are about relationships, meanings, and stories. Transitions are internal, invisible, emotional, and psychological. They happen slowly and are uncontrollable and unpredictable.

This section is about understanding transitions and how to manage them.

The first person to write about emotional and psychological transitions was Arnold van Gennep. In the early 1900s he studied the rites of passage associated with the major life transitions of death, marriage, and the shift from childhood into adulthood. What he discovered was that we never go straight from State A into State B. There is always a third, intermediate, or transitional, stage where we are no longer in the old identity but not yet fully in the new one either. He called this stage the liminal zone, after the Latin word *limen* which means threshold. In this phase we are crossing the threshold from one identity to another. This is the chrysalis stage between the caterpillar and the butterfly.

Getting married provides a good example of the three stages. Traditionally a wedding is preceded by a period of engagement, when we start to let go in our minds of our old identity and come to terms with the idea that we are going to take on a new role. The wedding itself is then the transitional stage, when we cross the threshold and officially become 'married'. This is then followed by a period of time when we start to integrate, consolidate, and embody our new identity, and find out what being married really means for who we are and how we behave in the world. This is the honeymoon and beyond, when the work of becoming married really begins.

These three phases also exist whenever we start in a new job. There is a period between quitting our previous role and starting the new one, when we prepare for the changes that are coming and let go of who we used to be. Then there are the first few days as we cross the threshold (perhaps literally) into a new workspace, find our feet, and build new relationships. And once we have joined the dots, connected it all together, we find the inner confidence to start to shape and mould the results we want. (The same happens when we change schools.)

Van Gennep called these phases pre-liminary, liminary, and post-liminary. The names don't really matter. What matters is that we take appropriate actions to ease our way through the stages. So I am going to use the more descriptive terms of Separation (separating from the old life), Threshold (crossing the threshold), and Consolidation (building and combining the various parts of what your vision means).

Emotions being what they are, these three stages do not necessarily come in a nice neat order. We might find ourselves still longing for the old life, even while we are crossing the threshold or consolidating our understanding of the new vision. But the steps provide a framework that we can use to understand and facilitate the process. We start by learning to let go of whatever came before.

Phase One: Separating from the Previous Life

Why This Matters

The Separation stage is the period between handing in your resignation and starting a new job. It's the time between deciding to become a parent and the actual birth of your child. And when you move home, it's the packing up stage, recalling memories and meanings, and saying goodbye to the place you are about to leave.

Separation is the time when the decision to take on a new identity has been made, but the work of building that identity has not yet begun. It's the time when we turn from looking back to looking forward. We cannot move easily into the future if we are still holding on to the past, so separation is about enabling you and your team to let go of that past, in a useful way.

What this looks like for your particular project will vary depending on your circumstances. If you are launching a new startup then people are likely to join you with most of their Separation phase already completed: they've decided to let go of what they were doing before and join you instead. If you're making a career change then your 'team' will be your family and friends. They may find it difficult to separate from their old ideas about who they think you are. And if you are leading an existing organisation or team in a new direction then you may need to spend significant amounts of time assisting people to leave behind the legacy of what that organisation once meant to them, taking the best bits with them as they move forward.

Separation is about getting closure for part of our lives. And of course there is also your own separation to go through.

Letting go of emotional attachment to the past is at the heart of why Kodak failed. It was unable to let go of its identity as a chemical photographer and move into the digital age. Emotional attachment also explains why CEO Howard Schultz found it impossible to convince the owners of the company he worked for to stop selling coffee beans and equipment and start selling drinks instead. Before he could create the global brand we know today he had to form a new company and buy Starbucks from them.

Letting go of an old identity is key to forming a new one.

What to Do About It

The more that people have been inspired by your vision-story, the easier this separation will be for them. The vision acts as a magnet, pulling people forward.

But during the Separation stage, some people may still experience grief for what is being lost. This might seem like an overreaction but it is entirely appropriate for anyone who feels it. So if you find people displaying anger, denial that change is needed, bargaining to go back to the old ways, or depression, don't necessarily take these emotions at face value. Recognise instead that they may be signs that people are experiencing grief. Better to acknowledge those feelings than to bottle them up or deny them, which would likely only lead to their returning later, in unpredictable and potentially disruptive ways.

Your role as a leader at this point is to help yourself and your people to identify what you are losing, individually and collectively, then to let those things go in a way that enables you all to turn from looking back to facing forward. This might take only a few moments of quiet reflection. Or if you are leading large numbers of people in a new direction, it might evolve over several weeks and months.

What matters here is not so much the things that are being lost, but the meanings that these things hold for people. If we think about Maslow's hierarchy of needs, these could include a sense of safety or belonging, friendships, being part of a team, pride, purpose, and a sense of identity or achievement.

Turning the Problem into an Opportunity

Grief for the loss of the past can seem to be a roadblock that is preventing you from moving forward. But if you understand it differently, grief can become an opportunity. What feelings of grief and loss really mean is that something exists that is so important to people that they have not yet been able to let go of it. If you can identify what that is, and show them how it is being rebuilt as part of the new vision, then this becomes an opportunity for people to shift their attachment to the past into an even stronger commitment to your vision. This will help them to separate.

To help yourself and others move through separation, realise that the future you are going to create would not have been possible without the past. That past has brought you the skills, experience, and resources you are going to use. It has taught you what matters most, which has shaped the direction you have chosen. And, paradoxically, you can now leave that past behind and take it with you if you generate clear memories of what was best about it and renewed clarity on how you are going to apply and rebuild those things in the future. This is a time to revisit, update, and strengthen your vision-story.

As you do this, remember that grief and the other emotions associated with Separation are not rational so they cannot be resolved through purely rational means. Simply telling people logically that "the future will rebuild the past" is not enough.

Rituals and symbolic acts are important ways to show people as well as tell them that they are moving through the Separation phase. Simple actions such as holding a farewell party, making a speech, or giving a thank you gift can be ways to physically to act out the letting go and moving on. Retirement parties are one example.

The details depend on your situation. You might want to bury something, plant a tree, write a letter (but not send it), burn a symbolic object in a ritual way, or hold a minute's silence. People might want to take with them a physical memento of the past: a pebble, a signed card, a photograph, a plant.

Remember most of all that there is no single best way of doing this: there is only whatever is appropriate for you and the unique people around you. Your ability to connect authentically with what that is, and to speak that truth on behalf of yourself and others, is a critical part of your leadership at this stage. This uses the abilities you developed with the tools of Chapters 1 and 2 to connect deeply with yourself and make clear sense of the situation.

The Troubles of Northern Ireland provide a large-scale example. These were a deep-rooted inter-community conflict that lasted around thirty years, from the late 1960s until the Good Friday Agreement of 1998. Seventeen years on, in 2015, in Derry/Londonderry a giant wooden 'Temple' was built in honour of the more than 3,500 people who had died in the conflict. People placed mementos, messages, and photographs in the space. The structure was clad in intricate panels, some of which had been designed and cut by young people from the city. And at dusk on the 21st of March, the spring equinox, the point at which the days become longer than the nights, the Temple was set on fire. This was a symbolic, ritualistic way for people to separate from what had gone before, and move on.

Change is an opportunity to consciously identify what matters most to us and work to build that anew. Separation is about turning away from looking back to facing forward. Whether people are finding this easy or difficult, holding a ritual event is a useful way to mark the end of Separation. Crossing the threshold can then begin.

Tool One: Managing the Separation Phase

What separation looks like and how best to handle it will vary widely, depending on your situation. If you find it difficult to appreciate how others might be experiencing loss as you work towards your vision, stop and remember a time when you lost something or someone that was important to you. The difference between how you felt then and how you feel now highlights the benefits that achieving successful Separation and closure can bring.

Then use these four sets of questions to think through how you and your team might let go of the past and focus on the future. (The tools of Chapters 1 and 2 may also be useful.)

First, identify the key groups and individuals who are most important to achieving your vision. Are they different from the audiences you inspired in Chapter 6? Put yourself at the top of the list.

On a scale of 0 to 10 how fully has each group separated from what the past means to them? How do you know? Is lack of separation causing problems? What would it look like if people shifted fully to a 10?

What specifically does each group or person most value from the past? What do they not want to lose? What does that mean to them?

(Maslow's hierarchy of needs can be a useful starting point for thinking this through: safety, belonging, esteem or respect, self-actualisation or identity.)

How can you give thanks for what has been, accept that it cannot be regained, and show instead that this meaning can be rebuilt as part of the future vision? How does this reshape your vision-story for this group or individual?

What event or ritual might symbolise an ending of the old phase and a beginning of the new? When would be a good time for this? Where and how?

Phase Two: Crossing the Threshold

Why This Matters
Having let go of the past, you and your team can now start to build the future. This is the chrysalis stage between the caterpillar and the butterfly. The old structure has been lost but the new structure of your future vision has not yet formed.

As you work to convert your imagined vision into operational realities, the psychological and emotional process of crossing the threshold will bring a time of uncertainty. This might range from fear about whether the vision will actually ever be achieved to simply "getting the hang of the new way we do things around here."

What it looks like in practice will again depend on your specific situation and on the level of inspiration your vision-story has generated. In the "temporary wilderness" of this phase, people may find themselves feeling uncertain, disoriented, lonely, vulnerable, and afraid, especially if it lasts for any length of time.

What to Do About It
Your role now is to provide people with structure. But in a churning world this can't just be imposed, top-down. It has to be structure that people create, develop, and internalise for themselves.

There are two ways you can achieve this.

First, you can enable people to cope better with ambiguity and uncertainty by developing their capacities for inner leadership. Teach them the tools of Chapters 1 to 3 and they will be less affected by uncertainty and find more creative solutions to it. Teach them the tools of Chapters 4 and 6 and they will inspire themselves and others to step forward more fully into the Threshold.

Get people to see their challenges as opportunities. If people feel lonely, get them to talk to one another. It they feel uncertain because things are undefined, get them to define what they want instead. Teach people to use the tools of Chapter 3 to identify alternatives to the issues they face. Then keep those solutions flexible as you move forward, allowing them to evolve further as necessary. The Threshold phase is too soon to be asking, "Are we there yet?" Instead ask, "Are we moving in the right direction?"

Then, as well as enabling individuals to "put their own oxygen masks in place," you can also provide structure collectively. Management guru Peter Drucker wrote that, "Culture eats strategy for breakfast." You can provide a second layer of structure for your people by putting in place the culture of your finished vision.

To achieve this, identify the values that will make your vision succeed and why they are important. Then define the attitudes and behaviours that will bring those values alive in each part of your organisation. (We already saw, for example, how Apple has built its vision around a culture of "deep collaboration and cross-pollination… which allow us to innovate in a way that others cannot.")

Implementing this culture will bring the intangible half of your vision alive immediately, and accelerate the achievement of tangible goals. It will also support you and your team to move through the uncertainty of the Threshold phase. The outer world might be churning but you can define the values, attitudes, and behaviours you will adopt, no matter what happens.

One day you will look back at this Threshold stage as a time of freedom. So treat the uncertainty of this period as an opportunity for creativity, innovation, exploration, and adventure. Experiment. Focus on values combined with the stability and innovation that come from Chapters 1 to 3. In the Threshold stage all things are possible.

Tool Two: Crossing the Threshold

The details of your Threshold stage and how best to handle it will depend on your situation. Use these questions to identify ways for you and your team to move through the uncertainties of the chrysalis stage and use those uncertainties to strengthen your organisation.

Who are the individuals and groups who are most important to the success of your vision-project? On a scale of 0 to 10, how critically important is each of them? How strongly are they currently able to centre and ground, make sense of their situations, and find the opportunities in a crisis? What actions are appropriate, if any?

Identify the values that are important for your vision to succeed. Translate them into the values, attitudes, and behaviours that are appropriate for each part of your team. This provides guidance for responding to any situation and adds another layer of detail to your vision-story. Apple's vision (page 110) provides an example.

How effectively (0 to 10) have you communicated these values and behaviours, together with the reasons why they matter? How effectively (0 to 10) do you and your team demonstrate and embody those values and behaviours each day? Is it a priority to change this? What would be the impact(s) of changing these scores?

If you or members of your team are having difficulty dealing with uncertainty, ask yourself whether the root cause is because people do not understand the values and behaviours that are needed or because they are not putting them into practice. If putting the values into practice is the issue, would Chapter 3 enable people to find more alternative ways forward? Would Chapters 1 and 2 improve people's abilities to centre and ground and make sense of new situations?

If part of your team is having difficulties in the Threshold phase consider the issue *you* face in addressing this. What values apply to the way you will deal with this situation? Which of the ten options of Chapter 3 represents *your* best approach? How can you address this issue in a way that turns it into an opportunity to walk your talk and demonstrate the values that will bring the vision alive?

Phase Three: Consolidation

Why This Matters
Having successfully separated from the past and crossed the uncertainties of the Threshold phase, you and your team can now focus undistracted on implementation. Step by step you put in place the building blocks of your vision and start to deliver what you set out to achieve.

For Uber, these building blocks included launching the first version of its app, then signing up drivers city by city. For Amazon, they were about putting in place systems and agreements to sell books in the USA, then expanding into more product lines and more countries.

During this time what is happening for people psychologically and emotionally is two things. First, they are gaining reassurance and confidence that the plan is working and that your vision really will deliver what you said it would. Second, they are consolidating their various experiences of the project to form an integrated overall understanding or impression of what your vision means to them: this becomes the brand image or brand perception.

We all know today what Amazon, Uber, and Airbnb do. But once upon a time all three were radical, untried new business models. All three had to inspire people to Separate from the ways they previously bought books, hired cabs, and rented rooms. Then they had to convince customers, investors, and employees to stick with them through the uncertain Threshold phase. And only after they had moved through Consolidation did Amazon and Airbnb finally become the established corporations we know and trust today.

The events surrounding the firing of Travis Kalanick from Uber, on the other hand, provide a textbook example of what can happen when the Consolidation stage is managed poorly.

Successful completion of Consolidation brings a final layer of inspiration and emotional engagement to your colleagues, customers, suppliers, and investors. For other people it also brings the extra levels of confidence and engagement they need before they can become your next groups of customers, employees, investors, and so on.

When you reach the end of Consolidation you have achieved your vision. You have created something new in the world and at the same time learned new ways of understanding and shaping that world. This is true of every transition you have completed in your life.

The first time it happened was the day that you were born. Your mother's contractions formed the Separation phase, preparing you for the changes that were coming. The birth itself was the Threshold. And then, out in this strange new world, you Consolidated the transition by learning the profoundly new skills of breathing and eating, and making sense of the world through your five senses more clearly than you had ever done before. You had no control over any of this, and yet you accomplished it seamlessly. And then you moved on to the next sets of changes and transitions: learning to walk and talk, make friends, go to school, ride a bike, drive a car, form relationships, get a job, and so on.

With each transition you learned new skills for influencing the world and a gained deeper understanding.

What this time of enormous change and churning offers you is the chance to develop the new skills and understanding that matter most to you.

What to Do About It

To help people pass through their emotional consolidation process, focus on two things: showing them that progress is being made and shaping what that progress means to them. Use these five steps.

The first step is to achieve quick wins. Each success shows that progress is being made. Small steps also bring flexibility to respond to events. Schedule them into your plan.

The second is to celebrate those successes. Make sure that people know and appreciate what has happened. Show how the vision is moving forward, and use each communication as an opportunity to shape what it means for your different audiences. Chapter 1 already showed two simple ways of achieving this: thanking and praising people for what they have done and spending time at the end of each day to review your progress. For larger milestones, symbolic acts such as cutting a cake or ribbon and other forms of celebration will also be appropriate.

Third, have a plan. Operationally this is obvious. Emotionally it provides focus and reassurance. When people see that something is part of a wider plan, each achievement becomes part of building something larger and makes future steps seem more likely to come true.

Fourth, join the dots. Be consistent. Show how everybody has a role to play and how each part matters. Recognise that while people are developing their understanding of what the vision means to them, every choice you and your team make can have an impact. A decision made by a person building the Uber app can lead to frustration in a driver, which might create fear or annoyance in a customer, which then leads to a story in the press and impacts the performance of the marketing department. The shared values and culture you implemented during the Threshold phase will help people to make choices that build a consistent overall picture. During Consolidation, you can strengthen this consistency and make it more actionable by shifting the focus from values to purpose.

Fifth, use purpose not only to join the dots but to enable coherent responses to new situations. As you move forward, things will not always go according to plan. Purpose provides a way to know what matters and what doesn't. It helps you find alternative routes to similar outcomes. And purpose provides faster, clearer decision-making, better focus, motivation, flexibility, and results. All of these help to maintain momentum and consistency during the Consolidation phase.

If the opportunity you chose in Chapter 4 was to achieve a specific outcome, the Consolidation stage will finish once that end is in sight. (The team will then enter a Separation phase in preparation for the next project.)

If you chose to build a new organisation, Consolidation finishes once it stops being a project and starts being a viable ongoing enterprise. Then it can shift and evolve in response to changing market conditions, in the way that Amazon (once it was established/ consolidated) expanded from books into clothing and household goods, then web services, and now television production. Who knows where Uber, Airbnb, or SpaceX might one day evolve to?

Wherever your organisation goes, each diversification will involve another pass through the steps of inner leadership: making sense of the situation, finding the best way forward, creating a new vision, and re-crossing the three stages of transition as you implement.

If we look back through this section on transitions, we can see that during the Separation stage your Vision-Story provides a reason for people to switch from looking backwards to looking forwards; Values provide a guiding framework for passing through the uncertainty of the Threshold stage; and Purpose develops this and makes it more actionable as you carry out Consolidation. And what enables people to put all of this into action is their own individual capacity for personal inner leadership.

The overall vision, values, and purpose *pull* the organisation forward. They provide top-down focus, consistency, and flexibility.

Personal inner leadership *pushes* the organisation forward. It provides the bottom-up resilience, responsiveness, energy, and inspiration needed to make it all happen.

Combined in this way, organisations and people have the potential to form a resilient, adaptable whole that can adapt and evolve in whatever ways the economy develops.

We will look more closely at the implications and consequences of this in Chapter 8.

Tool Three: Managing Consolidation

The details of the Consolidation stage will vary depending on your circumstances. Use these questions to identify how you and your team can best maintain inspiration, enthusiasm, and emotional engagement during the Consolidation stage, and ensure that what people experience matches the original intention of your vision-story.

Define the milestones (large and small) on the way to your vision. Include quick wins.

Define which audiences will care about which milestones, and why.

Define a communications plan: what you will communicate to which audiences, when, and how. How will you monitor whether these communications are achieving the outcomes you want?

What are the benefits of informing the key groups and individuals you rely on about the overall plan? How well is that being achieved today (0 to 10)? What actions if any are appropriate to address that? When will you take them?

How clearly do the members of your team understand the roles and contribution they each make in the achievement of the overall project? How clearly do they understand the contributions and dependencies of others? Does the purpose of the project motivate and inspire them? Do they use that purpose in their daily decision-making? Is it appropriate to develop a specific purpose statement for any groups or individuals? What actions are appropriate to develop and communicate the overall purpose?

How will you know when the Consolidation stage is complete? What milestones remain until you reach that point? What changes to culture, attitudes, and behaviour would most affect the successful achievement of that outcome?

What comes next after Consolidation?

Inspiring New Recruits

In a world that is churning, almost everyone you meet will be in one of the three stages of transition. Remembering this can be useful when recruiting new members to your team, whether as employees, suppliers, customers, or investors.

If these people understand transitions and are managing their own inner leadership process then all well and good. If not, then focus on vision, values, and purpose.

If the person is in their Separation stage then talk to them about your vision. If it brings them a chance to rebuild what matters most to them then they will be motivated to support your project. If not, then no matter what their skills or resources, their motivation to support your vision will always be low.

If a person is in their Threshold phase, uncertain, talk to them about values. If their values align with yours then your project may provide a way for them to work through their Threshold and make new meaning for themselves. If not then, no matter what their skills or resources are, they will always be a disruptive influence because when the issue of the day arises the values they use to shape their decisions will always be different from yours.

Apple's 2014 shareholder meeting provides an example. A shareholder asked CEO Tim Cook about the profitability of Apple's various environmental initiatives, such as its solar-powered data centre. Cook growled back, "We do things for other reasons than a profit motive, we do things because they are right and just. I don't think about the bloody ROI. Just to be very straightforward with you, if that's a hard line for you… you should get out of the stock." This reply is not driven by strategy, execution, or financial returns, nor by purpose, mission, or vision. It is deeply rooted in values.

If people are in their Consolidation phase, working to build a vision of their own, then talk to them about purpose. The more aligned their purpose is with yours, the more you will be able to count on each other's support, no matter what happens. The less aligned you are, the more you can expect to have ongoing disagreements and conflicts, because whatever the issue of the day, your purposes, your priorities, the destinations you are travelling towards will be different.

The more you can find partners who are aligned with you in vision, values, and purpose, and the more consciously aware of this you all are, the more likely it is that you will assemble a team that remains passionately committed to supporting your vision over the long term. Because in building your vision each person will also be building their own inner leader: building themselves.

A Map to Guide You

Before setting out on their journeys, the great explorers of old would always try to get hold of a map of the landscapes they were about to enter. Where were the swamps and deserts? Where was the fresh water and plentiful food? Rumours and stories from people who had been there or somewhere similar before were always useful. Even a sketch map was better than no map at all.

No one has ever tried to create your vision before, not in the way that you have defined it, and not in the circumstances you now face. But in your journey through *Inner Leadership* you have explored much of the inner territory you are about to enter. By pulling together the key landmarks you can prepare yourself for what will come next.

In times when you seem to be lost you will be able to refer to these landmarks, reorient yourself, and continue your journey forward.

The *Inner Leadership Workbook* contains a large format version, the electronic workbook contains a printable version, or you can easily recreate this list yourself. (Relevant chapters are shown in brackets.)

Explorers entering new territory would expect to encounter bad weather, difficult terrain, unhelpful people, and resource shortages. Having this map of landmarks with you when you encounter similar difficulties will enable you quickly to remember your priorities, renew your focus, and move forward to find the good weather, easy terrain, helpful people, and resources you need to reach your vision. They do exist, and you will encounter them as well. And like any good explorer, you can update your map as you move forward.

The second volume of this book, *Outer Leadership*, will provide tools and frameworks for putting your priorities into practice.

Map of Key Landmarks
(To be used for reorientation, as needed)

- Name ....   Date ....

Purpose and Values (Chapter 5)
- My purpose is to ....
  ....

- The values that are important to me in achieving that are
  ...., ..., and ....

Opportunity (Chapter 3, 4)
- The opportunity I have chosen as the best way to achieve that
  purpose now is ....
  ....

My Vision of that opportunity (Chapter 6)
- Authenticity for me is about ....

- My audience is looking for ....

- The reality of the situation is that ....

- I can convince my audience to make a decision now by ....

- Relevant higher principles, values, ideals ....

- The future we are going to create is ....

- And the first steps (which we know we can do) are ....

Managing the Journey (Chapter 7)

- Key individuals and groups important to my vision ....
  ....
- Transition stage they are currently in ....
  ....
- My focus for each group ....
  ....

Oxygen Masks (Chapter 1, 2)

- When I encounter churning, I centre and ground myself by
  ....
- I anchor myself by ....
  ....
- I refresh/deepen my connection with myself by ....
  ....
- Quotes that inspire me ....
  ....
- Motivators and facts that spur me to action ....
  ....

What It Will Take for Me to Have Lived a Worthwhile Life
and what I am doing about it this week/month (Chapter 4)

Focus Area:	Action, When:
1.	....
2.	....
3.	....
4.	....
5.	....
6.	....
7.	....
8.	....

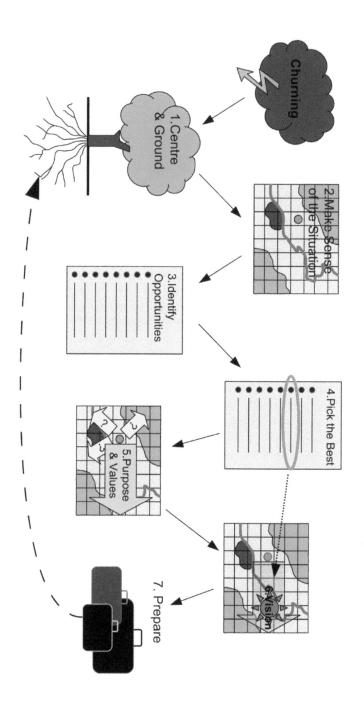

Inner Leadership Overview

Conclusions

If you have experienced any churning while reading this chapter, remember to use the tools of Chapter 1 to centre and ground.

As you start to implement your vision, you and your people will move through three stages of psychological and emotional transition.

In the first stage you separate from the past and turn to face the future. To achieve this more quickly, give thanks for what the past has brought you, accept that it has gone, and focus on your vision of how you are now going to rebuild what matters most. Mark the end of the Separation stage in a ritualistic way.

The second stage is to cross the Threshold. In this chrysalis stage the old structure has been lost but the new structure of your vision has not yet formed. What matters here is to provide frameworks for dealing with ambiguity and uncertainty. Top-down, you can do this by defining the culture of your finished vision, expressed as values, attitudes, and behaviours. Bottom-up, the tools of inner leadership enable individuals to manage their own responses to uncertainty in productive, generative ways that bring more options and inspiration.

The third stage is Consolidation. The aims in this phase are to maintain enthusiasm and emotional engagement and to build coherence between the different parts of the project and the original intent of the vision-story. Key success factors here are communication and focus on shared purpose.

The final section of this chapter pulled together key landmarks from your journey through *Inner Leadership* and used them to create a sketch map that you can take with you on the journey to your vision: reminders that you can use to align and realign yourself from time to time.

You have now completed the tools and framework for leading yourself and others to create inspiration during this time of change. You are ready to shift to *Outer Leadership*: leading for results.

As you implement your chosen way forward, issues will arise. Each will be a opportunity for you to reapply the tools of inner leadership. As you do so you will gain confidence and speed. Chapter 8 describes three additional levels of benefit that you can then expect to gain as a result.

Measurement

On a scale of 0 to 10, how well-prepared are you now to maintain your own inspiration and that of your team as you journey towards the outcome you chose in Chapter 4? How does this compare with where you were at the start of the chapter?

What differences will this make in your life? What benefits will that bring? How valuable is that to you?

Is it a priority for you to strengthen these abilities further? Why? How much time will you allocate to achieving this?

Or are you now ready to move to *Outer Leadership*?

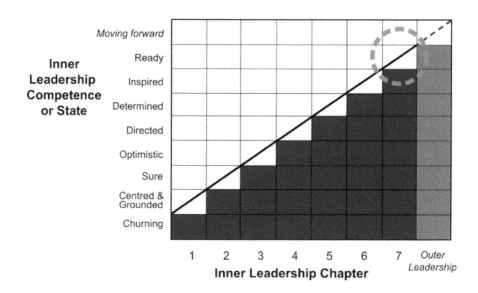

8. IMPLICATIONS AND CONSEQUENCES

This book has given us a set of tools for building inspiration and emotional engagement during times of change. Used together, these tools provide a framework for making us better leaders, both of ourselves and other people.

This chapter looks at what happens when we keep using these tools repeatedly over time.

In the Introduction I said this would bring us three more levels of benefit. In order of increasing scale they are: joy for us as individuals, antifragile competitive advantage for our organisations, and a new, more stable, less volatile economy.

We start with joy.

Joy

We have created a world that is volatile, uncertain, complex, and ambiguous. So much change is happening so fast that it sometimes seems as if anything might happen, and occasionally it does. But from the day that you were born your life has always involved change. From learning to walk and talk to going to school, from riding a bike and driving a car to getting your first job, moving home, making new friends, forming relationships, earning promotions, and dealing with new issues, your whole life has always been about change and transitions. Stability is an illusion. The only difference now is that more change is happening more quickly than we are used to, and more of that change is being created by people who live far away from us – all of which makes our transitions more difficult to predict and control.

So what does it mean when *everything* is changing?

Philosopher Alan Watts told us that the meaning of the fact that everything around us is dissolving constantly is that it frees us to let go – because there is nothing to hold on to.

When we realise this and accept it we can stop "wasting energy all the time in self-defence, trying to manage things, trying to force things to conform to [our] will."

"The moment you stop doing that," Watts says, "that wasted energy is available... you are one with the Divine Principle... [And when] you really get with that, suddenly you find you have the power, this enormous access of energy... power with which you can be trusted."

This is the joy I spoke about in the Introduction. It brings another layer of stability, determination, inspiration, drive, and momentum for achieving whatever matters most.

Inner Leadership enables us to access this joy in two ways.

First, it defines our purpose and values in terms of what makes us feel most alive, our best qualities, and the ways we love using them. When we live and work in line with purpose and values defined this way we will inevitably experience joy.

Second, *Inner Leadership* provides a safety net to catch us every step of the way. This frees us to let go. Because no matter what happens, we know we will be able to steady ourselves, make clear sense of the situation, find more opportunities, and turn the best of them into an inspiring vision, managing our transitions as we go forward.

When we combine these two things – combine purpose and values with tools for achieving greater innovation, flexibility, and inspiration – then we obtain the joy of striving for what matters most to us. We achieve what the ancient Greeks called *eudaimonia*, fulfilment, joy.

In grounded modern psychological terms, this is about connecting more deeply with who we are and what we care about, and increasing our ability to put that into practice in the world. This is called individuation or self-actualisation.

We cannot control our world. We never could. But we what we can do is find the stability and joy we seek, *inside* ourselves. *Inner Leadership* gives us the tools to achieve that: to find the best way forward for us and put it into practice, no matter what situation we find ourselves in.

In case that seems unlikely, consider bomb-torn Baghdad. Here, in April 2015, a car packed with explosives detonated in the busy Mansour district, killing at least ten people and injuring 27. Is it really possible for someone to live in line with their purpose and values under such circumstances?

Karim Wasfi, renowned conductor of the Iraqi National Symphony Orchestra, decided that it was. He took his cello and went to play at the site of the explosion. When asked why, he replied:

> "It's partially the belief that civility and refinement should be the lifestyle that people should be consuming... It was an action to try to equalise things, to reach the equilibrium between ugliness, insanity, and grotesque, indecent acts of terror – to equalise it, or to overcome it, by acts of beauty, creativity, and refinement."

So the act of playing the cello was the opposite to the act of detonating a bomb?

> "Yes, creating life basically... Life [in Baghdad] is experienced on a daily basis, even though we don't experience normalcy. When things are normal, I will have more responsibilities and obligations. But when things are insane and abnormal like that I have the obligation of inspiring people, sharing hope, perseverance, dedication, and preserving the momentum of life."

Even in the most extreme circumstances there is always something we can do.

Aung San Suu Kyi applied this philosophy during her decades-long fight for democracy in her country. "My attitude," she said, "is, do as much as I can while I'm still free. And if I'm arrested I'll still do as much as I can."

Viktor Frankl survived the Nazi concentration camps. Reflecting afterwards on what had enabled people to live through them, he realised that people who lost their sense of purpose tended to get sick and then die. But people who felt that "life was still expecting something from them; something in the future was expected of them" were able to make meaning of their lives, even under those appalling conditions. Making that meaning, he said, gave people "the last of the human freedoms – to choose one's attitude in any given set of circumstances, to choose one's own way." For Frankl, this was what made the difference between life and death.

In a time of churning we can't always choose what happens to us but we can choose how we respond.

If we know the values that make us feel most fully alive and the kind of world we want to create (our purpose), if we know how to find more opportunities in a situation and how to manage our transitions as we put the best of them into practice, then we give ourselves the freedom and the power to do as much as we can, to make our own meaning, to choose our own way, to individuate and self-actualise. We enable ourselves to pursue what Peter Drucker called "the only worthy goal – to make a meaningful life out of an ordinary one."

When we live in line with our purpose and values, and use the other tools to put them into practice, then we free ourselves to let go of what does not matter to us and focus instead on what does. We become "one with the Divine Principle" and experience an "enormous access of energy… power with which [we] can be trusted."

This is what I meant by joy, and practicing the tools of *Inner Leadership* enables us to achieve it.

Antifragile Competitive Advantage

The second outcome I predicted was that inner leadership would bring competitive advantage for our organisations and would make them antifragile. How does this come about?

The mechanisms by which inner leadership generates competitive advantage are now clear: a churning world forces organisations to change and each change forces people to transition. People with strong inner leadership capabilities are able to handle these transitions more easily. They also stay calmer when the next change arises, find more options for moving forward, and quickly turn the best of them into an inspiring vision. Organisations whose people are skilled at inner leadership react better and faster to change, and implement more inspiring responses that last longer. In a churning world this brings competitive advantage.

But what about antifragility? How does inner leadership enable organisations to handle change in a way that actually makes them stronger?

To understand this, let's first walk step by step through the essence of what happens during one cycle of organisational change. Let's identify the fundamentals so that we can pinpoint what it takes to lead the process more effectively. Then let's look at how to turn that into antifragility.

The diagram below provides a summary.

Change at any scale begins when one person notices a pattern of events, either inside or outside the organisation. They decide it means that change might be needed (either as a 'problem' or an 'opportunity') and raise the issue to the organisation. This is Box 1.

If the organisation agrees the issue is important it then makes plans to address the matter. This is Box 2.

Box 3 is execution. The organisation implements its change plan.

Each person affected by the change then goes through a psychological and emotional transition. Some of these will be small, others large. This is Box 4.

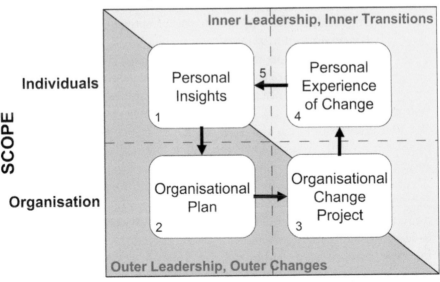

And, for better and for worse, the experiences of these transitions then reshape the world views of each affected person, either confirming more deeply what they already knew or teaching them something new about the way the world works. This is Arrow 5.

The next time these people find themselves facing an issue that might require change (back to Box 1 again) they will use these new world views and insights, and their learning from what happened last time, to decide whether to speak up and how to go about doing so.

Charting this process, from planning to execution, from individual to organisation, from inner to outer leadership and back again, gives us a picture I call the 'Cycle of Leadership'. This is how change happens in organisations.

Any organisation that wants to succeed in a churning economy needs to be able to move rapidly, repeatedly, and consistently around this cycle.

Doing this well requires the organisation to have five key skills, competencies, or capabilities:

1. Leaders and people who are able to identify and prioritise issues, and surface them appropriately
2. Teams able to plan and predict the consequences of different courses of action in a churning world
3. Teams and a receptive organisation who are able to implement change programmes efficiently and effectively, with appropriate balance between inspiration and results
4. Leaders and people who are able to manage their transitions
5. A culture that uses each completed cycle of change to reinforce and develop its core purpose, values, attitudes, and behaviours

All organisations are the sum of all their people. So the more people in an organisation have these five skills, the more easily that organisation as a whole will be able to adapt.

Management guru Tom Peters told us that, "Leaders don't create followers, they create more leaders." In a time of change, this becomes more important than ever. The more people in an organisation are able to lead themselves and others using these five competencies, the more the organisation as a whole will be able to dodge and weave in response to change, like a flock of birds or a shoal of fish. This is why the two volumes of *The Churning* are focused on enabling everyone to develop these five critical competencies: to accelerate the process of creating lasting change in a churning world.

So how do these competencies make an organisation antifragile?

The first four are hopefully familiar to you. Let's look more closely at the fifth: 'a culture that uses each completed cycle of change to reinforce and develop its core purpose, values, attitudes, and behaviours.' This is the critical step that closes the loop. Without this step, an organisation might respond successfully to one change, but it won't improve its ability to deal with the next. In a time of constant change this matters.

For example, imagine an organisation that says it encourages risk-taking but in reality only gives bonuses to people who meet their financial targets. That organisation might move successfully through the first four steps but it will fail at the fifth to complete the loop. Instead of learning to take risks and innovate, the people will learn from experience not to believe what they are told. This will make them unsure and unwilling about confronting new issues (Steps 1 and 2) and more resistant to future changes (Steps 3 and 4). Over time the organisation's ability to respond to change will degrade.

But an organisation that shows consistency, and acts in line with its stated purpose and values, closes the loop in Step 5. What happens next is a kind of magic.

By actively using its purpose and values to shape its daily behaviour and decisions, the organisation teaches its people by example. It *shows* them what is important, not just with words but with actions. This consistency generates greater confidence and deeper understanding about which issues matter and how to raise them (Step 1). It helps people to more quickly design new plans (Step 2), implement them (Step 3), and handle the resulting transitions (Step 4).

In other words, by defining a set of purpose and values, and putting them at the heart of its daily operations and decision-making, the organisation *increases its ability to change and adapt.*

Then, after each change, as part of Step 5, the organisation gets the opportunity to develop and reinforce its purpose and values. First, it gets to understand and embed them more deeply, as people learn from experience how they applied in the situation the organisation just lived through. Second, it gets to refine them and the ways they are articulated: as purpose and values and as the attitudes and behaviours by which these are put into practice throughout the organisation.

This is where the antifragility arises.

Addressing an issue in isolation brings speed. But an organisation that takes the time to define the underlying purpose and values that shape its choices brings a focus and clarity that accelerate and facilitate the next cycle of change: making it easier to know which issues to ignore, which to address, and bringing a wider range of solutions to fruition more quickly and inspiringly.

This brings competitive advantage.

And each subsequent cycle of change then brings the opportunity to strengthen that advantage still further: embedding the purpose and values more deeply and improving the ways they are put into practice.

In this way, an organisation that practices *Inner Leadership* uses the 'stress' of each change to make itself stronger, both in knowing what it stands for and being able to put that into practice. Stability, focus, and growth are the result.

This is antifragility.

It is the ultimate competitive advantage, true sustainability.

It is the organisational equivalent of joy.

Two Examples – Google and Apple

Both Google and Apple have taken the time and gone to considerable effort to define their desired values, attitudes, and behaviours.

We know from Chapter 6 that Apple prides itself on having the "self-honesty to admit when we're wrong and the courage to change." The company also fosters "deep collaboration, cross-pollination, and innovation."

Google is well-known for creating exceptional work environments. Its values include "creating an environment where people can flourish and grow, treating people with fairness and respect, challenging each other's ideas openly, and valuing diversity in people and ideas."

By defining not what outcomes to seek but *how* to go about finding them, these ideals give both firms the inner stability to handle outer change. This has helped both to grow from small beginnings to become the world's most valuable brands.

A Stable Generative Economy

Now let's see what happens when people who are experiencing the joy of having 'let go' come to work in organisations that are run to be antifragile.

In very practical terms we can expect that people with the extra energy, focus, and flexibility that come from letting go will bring the organisations they work in higher quality, greater resilience, lower costs, faster time frames, and a greater ability to adapt. The organisations will benefit from wider spans of control and be more proactively self-organising, more networked, more like a swarm of living organisms.

The antifragile organisations, in turn, will provide their people with a consistent, supportive, inspiring environment. Each challenge the organisation faces will become an opportunity for those people to apply their purpose and values, find more alternative ways forward, and put the best of them into practice in an inspiring way. As they do so they will, in the words of Google, "flourish and grow." They will become better at putting their best qualities into practice in the ways they most love.

Some people will develop the new products and services the organisation needs. Others will come up with new forms of supply chain or delivery channel, or new forms of relationship with customers, suppliers, employees, or investors. Others will focus on implementing and delivering these innovations or on finding new ways to combine and coordinate them to shape the evolving direction of the firm.

In a churning world all these innovations are needed. Without them the organisation dies. And *by encouraging each person to "follow their heart" the organisation becomes most likely to develop and apply the transformative innovations that will bring the greatest new value and be hardest for others to copy.*

Working together in this way, organisation and people become generative: they each grow the other. The people take the actions that grow the organisation. The organisation provides a 'container' that grows the people, so they flourish and become capable of even more.

I call this 'igniting the organisation'. Together, joyful people and antifragile organisation become a kind of mechanism for bringing their shared purpose and values alive in the world – then developing new ways of doing so as they respond to changing customer needs, emerging technologies, new moves by competitors, and so on.

The more the organisation is run to be antifragile, the more it uses each change to become stronger. The more the people have 'let go', the more transformative energy they bring to accelerate each change.

What happens next, as Paul Polman (CEO of Unilever) has described, is that new suppliers seek to join this generative, purpose-driven enterprise. And as they follow its lead so they, too, become antifragile: developing their abilities to apply their best qualities, in service to the larger business ecosystem (which then nurtures and grows them in return). In Unilever's case, it has seen its 'sustainable living' brands growing 30% faster than the rest of its business.

As this purpose-driven, generative ecosystem grows, so the economy as a whole becomes more stable and more generative. And in a knowledge economy, where value is no longer tied to resource usage, this has the potential to create infinite growth on a finite planet: not infinite in physical terms but infinite in terms of value created.

In case this seems unlikely, consider blockchain. Back in 2007 a person calling themselves Satoshi Nakamoto decided to follow their heart and develop a new way of arranging zeros and ones. They wrote a computer program, told an inspiring vision-story about what it meant (inventing the ideas of 'mining' for 'coins' of 'cryptocurrency'), and inspired so many people to agree with them that by the end of 2017 Bitcoin alone was worth almost $300 billion. Repeat innovations like this (more stably) across a generative, antifragile business ecosystem, and you have a glimpse of what is possible.

The process has already begun. Companies like Google are already giving employees the autonomy to pursue what interests them, then commercialising the best of whatever emerges. Companies like Tesla and SpaceX are already using inspiration to get more done with less.

The reason they are doing this is because it works. In a time of change, inspiration matters. Gallup's data proves this.

Every section of this book is already happening somewhere. What this book seeks to do that is new is to make the process explicit: to show the steps that are needed; to join the dots and provide tools that enable everyone to create organisations that succeed by maximising individual human potential and joy; and to combine that with antifragile competitive advantage – starting with ourselves.

If we want to end this time of volatility, uncertainty, complexity, and ambiguity, and shift to something better, we need a new kind of leadership. This book contains new thinking, frameworks, and tools for leading ourselves and other people to get there.

EPILOGUE

We started this book by saying this time of churning would require us to find new ways to lead ourselves and others. We have seen that if we apply these new tools then we become able to do more than just find a better way forward in a crisis: we learn to build ourselves a safety net that enables us to 'let go', find joy, create antifragile organisations, and build a more stable and generative economy.

As we end this book together, I cannot know what situation you are facing. I cannot know what will be the best way forward for you. Perhaps, like Elon Musk, you will choose to start a company to ensure the survival of the human race. Perhaps, like Aung San Suu Kyi in the 1980s, you will choose to fight for an issue you care deeply about, not knowing whether you will succeed or how long it will take. Or perhaps, like Karim Wasfi, you will pick up your cello and take it to a place where it needs to be played.

In effect, that is what all three of these people did: they found what was closest to their hearts, what mattered most to them, their purpose and their values, and then they gave themselves the freedom and the power to do what they could, with the resources they had, to inspire other people to do what needed to be done.

So, use this book to find your cello and your place to play it, your 'Carnegie Hall'. Identify the values that make you feel most fully alive and the purpose that aligns them. Find alternatives and choose whichever is the most appropriate way forward for you now. Then build the inspiration to make it happen, learn, improve, and repeat.

In a time of churning there is no telling where this will lead. And there are people longing to hear your song.

Further Reading

If you want to learn more about some of the ideas discussed in this book (and others omitted for reasons of space) you might find the following useful.

Books

Antifragile: Things that Gain from Disorder. Nassim Nicholas Taleb. Penguin, London, England, 2013.

The Artist's Way: A Course in Discovering and Recovering Your Creative Self. Julia Cameron. Pan Books, London, England, 1995.

Blink: The Power of Thinking Without Thinking. Malcolm Gladwell. Penguin, London, England, 2006.

The Effective Executive. Peter Drucker. Heinemann, London, England, 1967.

The Feeling Good Handbook (Revised Edition). David D Burns MD. Plume Books, New York, New York, 1999.

The Fifth Discipline: The Art and Practice of the Learning Organization. Peter M Senge. Random House Business (Second Edition), London, England, 2006.

The Human Element: Productivity, Self-Esteem and the Bottom Line. Will Schutz. Jossey-Bass, San Francisco, California, 1994.

The King Within: Accessing the King in the Male Psyche. Robert Moore & Douglas Gillette. William Morrow and Company Inc, New York, 1992.

The Leadership Dojo: Build your Foundation as an Exemplary Leader. Richard Strozzi-Heckler. Frog Books, Berkeley, California, 2007.

Managing Transitions: Making the Most of Change (Second Edition). William Bridges. Nicholas Brealy Publishing, London, England, 2003.

Man's Search for Meaning. Viktor E Frankl. Beacon Press, Boston, Massachusetts, 2006.

Non-Violent Communication: A Language of Life. Marshall B Rosenberg. PuddleDancer Press, Encinitas, California, 2003.

Patton, Montgomery, Rommel: Masters of War. Terry Brighton. Crown Publishing Group, New York, New York, 2009.

The Problem is the Solution: A Jungian Approach to a Meaningful Life. Marcella Bakur Weiner and Mark B Simmons. Jason Aronson, Lanham, Maryland, 2009.

A Return to Love: Reflections on the Principles of a 'Course in Miracles'. Marianne Williamson. Thorsons Publishing Group, London, England, 1996.

The Scottish Himalayan Expedition. WH Murray. Dent Publishing/The Orion Publishing Group, London, England, 1951.

The Seven Habits of Highly Effective People: Powerful Lessons in Personal Change. Stephen R Covey. Simon & Schuster, London, England, 1989.

Story: Substance, Structure, Style, and the Principles of Screenwriting. Robert McKee. ReganBooks (HarperCollins), New York, 1999.

Surfing the Edge of Chaos: The Laws of Nature and the New Laws of Business. Richard T Pascale, Mark Millemann and Linda Gioja. Texere Publishing Ltd, London, England, 2000.

The Rites of Passage. Arnold van Gennep. University of Chicago Press, Chicago, Illinois, 1961.

The Tao of Pooh. Benjamin Hoff, Penguin, London, 1983.

Ubiquity: The Science of History... or Why the World is Simpler than We Think. Mark Buchanan. Weidenfeld and Nicolson, London, England, 2000.

Websites

Alan Watts, "Creating Who You Are"
https://www.youtube.com/watch?v=Hu5oaty0uJM

A Better Kind of Happiness (How living on purpose affects genes)
http://www.newyorker.com/tech/elements/a-better-kind-of-happiness

The Drucker Institute
http://www.druckerinstitute.com

Elon Musk's blog announcement releasing Tesla's patents
http://www.teslamotors.com/en_GB/blog/all-our-patent-are-belong-you

Jack Canfield's Life Purpose Exercise
http://jackcanfield.com/are-you-living-your-passion/

Julia Cameron's Morning Pages tool
http://juliacameronlive.com/basic-tools/morning-pages/

The Sedona Method
http://www.sedona.com

Steve Jobs Commencement Address at Stanford, June 12 2005.
http://news.stanford.edu/news/2005/june15/jobs-061505.html

ABOUT THE AUTHOR

Finn Jackson is a coach, consultant, and speaker on strategy and leadership in times of change.

His experience of designing and implementing practical strategic change includes competitor analysis and strategic profit improvement for a boutique strategy consulting firm, and leading top to bottom strategic change across three continents as part of the European leadership teams of two of the top three global accounts at technology services company, EDS.

His straightforward approach to managing inner change and creating inspiration is deeply grounded in the work of Carl Jung, Gregory Bateson, Marshall Rosenberg, and others. It has been road tested through personal experiences that include divorce, bereavement, and serious illness.

Reviewers called his first book, *The Escher Cycle*, "A unified theory of business" that "describes business as a living system" and "offers a blueprint for winning any game your business chooses to play."

Born in Darjeeling, North East India, Finn has a degree in physics from Oxford University and an MBA with distinction from Imperial College, London. His values are honour, harmony and empowerment. His purpose is to create a generative world.